MY Heart
IN MY MOUTH

PRAYERS FOR OUR LIVES

TED LODER

WIPF & STOCK · Eugene, Oregon

Wipf and Stock Publishers
199 W 8th Ave, Suite 3
Eugene, OR 97401

My Heart in My Mouth
Prayers for Our Lives
By Loder, Theodore W.
Copyright©2000 by Loder, Theodore W.
ISBN 13: 978-1-62564-030-7
Publication date 4/15/2013
Previously published by Augsburg Books, 2000

My Heart in My Mouth
is lovingly dedicated
to my sister,
Rosemary Alice Creel,

whose courage
enables her to persevere against great odds,

whose vitality
brightens and warms those around her,

whose devotion
as a teacher, wife, and mother
changed countless lives,
including mine.

Contents

Introduction 10

Prayers of Invocation 15
    We Come as We Are 16
    Breathe Deeply into Us 18
    Worn into a Hallowed Glow 20
    We Dare to Speak Your Name 22
    Hover Over Us 24

Prayers of Praise 27
    The Weave of Miracles 28
    The Surprises of Grace 29
    Wonders that Seize Our Hearts 30
    One Moment of Praise 31
    In the Silence Between Our Heartbeats 32
    The Deepest Wonder of All 34
    Grace Beyond Our Grasp 36

Prayers of Thanksgiving 37
    Beautiful Beyond All Telling 38
    Thankful Beyond Understanding 40
    There Is Yet Love 41
    Transform Our Gratitude into Courage 44

Prayers of Confession   47
    Deepen Our Longing into Trust   48
    Let the Healing Begin   49
    Come Now to Find Us   50
    You Know the Secrets   52
    Restore Our Souls to Singing   54
    Restore the Circle of Humanity   56
    Home at Last   58

Prayers of Petition   59
    Listen to the Longing   60
    Let Your Kingdom Be the North Star for Us   62
    Strengthen Us to Answer with Brave Hearts   64
    Go Deeper, Further with Us   66
    We Dare to Ask   68

Prayers of Reflection   71
    Hold Us in the Embrace of Mercy   72
    We Hunger for What You Offer   74
    Is This What It Means to Be Free?   76
    We Yearn to Return to You   81
    Be New to Us Once More   82
    Meet Us in the Unexpected Places   84

Pastoral Prayers   87
    Keen Our Awareness   88
    We Pray Because We Breathe   94

Prayers of Dedication   97
    Multiply Our Faith   98
    Teach Us Again and Again   99
    Keep Us in Your Fierce Love   100

Prayers for a Few Special Occasions   103
   ADVENT:
      We Watch and Wait for You   104
   ADVENT:
      Gentle Us Open   106
   MARTIN LUTHER KING, JR., SUNDAY:
      Keep Us Faithful to Your Dream   108
   A MUSIC SERVICE:
      Tune Us Again to Timeless, Timely Words   110
   A WEDDING:
      Thank You for This Weaving of Lives   112
   CONFIRMATION:
      They Are Gifts to Us   115

Narrative Prayers   119
   The Only Answer-Choice There Is   120
   This Wrestle Through the Night   126

Personal Prayers   133
   Help Me to Trust that Joy Is a Hint   134
   I Have Only So Much Time   138
   I Pray to Be Steeped in Silence   140
   Tutor Me Yet Again   141
   Go With Me, God   144
   Let Me Make Something of This Loss   148
   Teach Me How to Die   153
   I Watch, Wondering, for You   156

Acknowledgments

I want to thank those who put my heart in my mouth every day through lives that shock, amaze, support, and bless me to an extent far beyond anything I deserve and bestow upon me more than enough of redemptive judgment, grace, and beauty, even if there is nothing more for me. They are my beloved wife, Jan; my incredible children, Mark, David, Karen, and Thomas; their spouses, Nadya, Steve, Amina; my grandchildren, Lyle, Amanda, Marek, Kyle, Jake, Julia, and Aaron; my stepsons, Christopher and Jonathan; their wives, Valerie and Hillary; and my new step granddaughter, Sofya Hoshaiah. This family both generates my prayers and answers them.

In addition I thank the people of the faith family of First United Methodist Church of Germantown who challenged and nurtured me through my almost thirty-eight years with them, and who prayed and lived many of the prayers in this book; my colleagues in ministry over the years, Bob Raines, John Rice, Jerry Rardin, Joan Hemenway, Art Brandenburg, Jean Alexander, Judith Hubbling, George Alt, Michele Bartlow, Noah Reed, Jacqueline Sanders, Jim McIntire, Beth Stroud and, most uniquely, Dr. Ann Marie Donohue, who found us in her wandering and without ordination became a highly valued and beloved Staff Associate of longest tenure. To this list I add those closest friends I will not name but who know I carry them in my heart always.

And of course, my gratitude abides for my friend, gifted, patient editor and publisher, Marcia Broucek, with whom I've traveled through many wilderness times to quite enough green pastures. None of these are responsible for this book except that without them it might well not have found the light of day or any prayers' eyes.

Introduction

For me, the simplest definition of prayer is putting your heart in your mouth. From deep within, some plea or question or gladness geysers up to address a presence or power beyond our human limitations. There is an unadorned urgency, honesty, and immediacy about it. It puts your heart in your mouth. Often, the beginning of a prayer is nearly as inarticulate as a gargle—a word or two, such as "please" or "thank you," a sigh or a grunt, as when the wind is knocked out of you, a catch in the breath of shame or sorrow, a curse of despair, an awed lump in the throat, a winged whoop of ecstasy.

Since from the beginning prayer seems to be hardwired into us, it is not surprising that there is this essentially primordial quality to it. It is only later that words come to shape those deep experiences of awareness, need, and emotion (as distinct from sentiment, which are feelings poured over life rather than emerging from within it). Sometimes the words come quickly, sometimes slowly, sometimes not at all. But when they do come, the words are never wholly adequate to the experience because prayer takes us close to the mysterious boundary between time and eternity, the "thin place" between this world and God's kingdom where our words stumble and grope.

The first question, then, to ask of any prayer we put to words is how far does it take us into that urgent, honest, and immediate experience at the heart of prayer? Does the prayer honestly help put our hearts in our mouths? No matter how poetic or sincere or fervent or lovely or religious or venerable, if the prayers in public liturgies or private devotions do not do that, then the least to be said of them is that they are much less helpful and authentic than if they do. But the rest to be said of such prayers is spoken by the prophet Isaiah:

> *Because these people draw near*
> *   with their mouths,*
> *and honor me with their lips,*
> *   while their hearts are far from me,*
> *and their worship of me*
> *   is a human commandment*
> *   learned by rote;*
> *so I will again do*
> *   amazing things with this people,*
> *   shocking and amazing.*
> *   —Isaiah 29:13-14, NRSV*

Clearly Isaiah gives us a strong caution that God does more than read our lips. Yet the prophet adds a reassuring promise to the scathing judgment, and I, for one, am profoundly grateful for it. That promise gives us hope that whatever traces of hypocrisy and self-promoting piety there are in even the best of our prayers, they do not thwart God from doing shocking and amazing things with us and around us.

Don't you suppose, then, that Isaiah, along with Jesus and all of scripture, is telling us that our prayers should be rooted in discerning those shocking and amazing things far beyond "human commandments learned by rote" or prattled in solemn clichés? I believe so because then we will have our hearts in our mouths at all the borders where eternity is constantly rubbing thin and gauzy the boundary with time. Then we will be honoring God not just with our lips but with our hearts, with our very lives.

It is important to add that we will be honoring God not just with those parts of our lives we think, or are told, are acceptable to God (which really would be honoring God just with our lips) but honoring God with all that we are: persons of "broken and contrite hearts," as well as seeking, questioning, doubting, hoping, proud, strong, able, confused, smart, confusing, glad, and believing hearts. What makes us think God cannot or will not take the dark and difficult parts of us along with the bright and best, the dirty and rumpled along with the washed and pressed? Is not honesty more trustworthy than pretense? Is God's grace really not sufficient to respond to us as we are, not as we assume we ought to be? Is God's mercy so insufficient that we can or should try to withhold our secret stock of unbelief or betrayals or self-serving behaviors or disturbing struggles from One ". . . from whom no secrets are hid"?

In any case, you begin to understand my audacity, if not outright presumption, in titling this book *My Heart in My Mouth*. That title is less a claim than an intention. Whether in the liturgies for public worship, as some of these prayers were in their original form, or in the more pastoral, personal, and reflective prayers, I have tried to retrieve at least some intimations of those occasions of nearly primal urgent, honest, immediate outpouring to the power and presence of One past our human limitations. I have tried to reflect those shocking, amazing glimmers of God that all of us have—sometimes without realizing very clearly that is what they are.

So a second question to ask of any prayer put to words is how powerfully does it discern those shocking, amazing things God is doing with and among us *now* rather than only referring us to past deeds. Does the prayer gather up, discern, and interpret our experiences in honest, relevant ways?

Introduction

This is a hard question and deserves a fuller response than I can make in this space. But I would say that imagination is a key to discernment, and so to prayer, even to faith. Noble laureate physicist Richard Feynman wrote something that clarifies the point: "Our imagination is stretched to the utmost, not, as in fiction, to imagine things that are not really there, but just to comprehend those things which really *are* there." That is precisely what I think discernment and faith are about: imagining and trying to comprehend, to interpret things that really are there but which somehow we have been intimidated into avoiding or denying for fear of being labeled naïve or unsophisticated. It seems the quantum physicists and cosmologists are rediscovering the mystery and wonder, or, if you will, the shocking and amazing things going on in our universe and in our world, while too often we "religious types" are off picking blackberries and flat-lining our lives. Among other things, perhaps foremost among other things, prayer is about imagining things that really *are* there in our experiences and helping us imagine them, trust them, engage them as the gracious mysteries they are.

Although our experiences are always specifically personal and individual, as are our memories, and our interpretations and pondering of them, there are always similarities, commonalties, communal qualities to them as well. Our thoughts and ways are not God's thoughts and ways, but we do share most of them in common with each other. So, I hope the words of these prayers will help you find your imagination and often put your heart in your mouth, too, by gathering up, in some recognizable way, pinches and scraps of those quick two or three words, those sighs and grunts, pained curses and lumps in the throat, winged whoops and gargled whispers, and so open you and your heart to God, to yourself, to others—and to those ordinary yet shocking and amazing human experiences that take our breath away, then give it back in great, merciful, graceful gulps. I also hope these prayers will enable you to live and work, relate and risk, serve and play, imagine and pray in more humble, creative, faithful, honest, joyful ways.

Introduction

Finally, most of us have had the experience of writing something that turns out to be richer, more moving, more powerful than we thought we could bring off. When we go back and read what we have written, we wonder where in the world it came from. Certainly I have that wonder about much of what I write. Of course, some of it comes from this world, the world I live in, engage, watch, wonder about, struggle to find meaning in, am often shocked and amazed by. But not all the words, not all the power and revelation in them comes from me and my world. I believe with all my heart that they come from a source higher, wiser, more holy and far better than I can even imagine. I want to acknowledge that source here without in any way dishonoring Her\Him by attributing too much of what I have put into words in this book to that Holy One. That source simply remains for me a mystery to be lived with, in, and for—sometimes with frustration, frequently with elegant puzzlement, occasionally with anger and a sense of alienation. Yet it is a mystery to be constantly lived with in whatever way will convey to God, and before each other, our overwhelming gratitude, awe, and every ounce of trust and love we can muster. I hope, I pray, you will catch intimations of that living, awe, gratitude, and trust in this book.

Introduction

Prayers OF INVOCATION

We Come as We Are

God of fierce holiness,
    yet of tender mercy,
  we come to add our voices
    to the chorus of praise
      raised to you from mountains to seas,
        from deserts to prairies,
          cities to towns to farms,
  to the voice of the turtle dove
    heard again in our land,
      to wind and rain and stirring earth,
        to blossom and green,
          scented lilac and singing peeper,
  to lover and beloved,
    hider and seeker,
      loser and finder,
        prophet and dreamer,
  and to all the life of this fertile planet.

We come as we are—
  troubled and weary,
    grateful and grumpy,
      nervy and scared,
        partially whole, still broken,
          mostly closed, hopefully open,
  grateful for your promise
    that you accept us,
      caring for our cares,
        rejoicing in our joys,
    enlivening in our breathing,
      forgiving in our confessing,
        forbearing in our singing,

hearkening in our praying,
speaking even in our scurrying words.

In this hour,
and at least some of the hours to come,
mute the distractions
that clamor for our attention,
until, by the tugging of your Spirit,
we are led to the water of life you are,
and we feel and admit the burn of thirst,
dare the humility to drink,
and exercise the wisdom
to center on you,
and on the things that make for peace
within us and among us
and throughout the earth.

Move among us,
stir in our midst,
reside in the between of us
to renew our faith in you,
in each other, and in ourselves.
in truer proportion;
to inflame into passion and action
our love of you, our neighbor,
and our flawed yet precious selves
that we may be more free and frolicky
in the living of our lives;
to lighten the burdens we cling to
of pride, of anger,
of prejudice, rigidity, and fear
that we may be more bold and imaginative
in our service of justice and your kingdom;
through Jesus Christ our Lord. Amen.

We Come as We Are

Breathe Deeply into Us

O unwearying One
    who stalks us down all our days,
  bring us up short, now,
    and breathe deeply into us
  for we come breathless to you
    from fretful times and frangible relations,
      our attention distracted,
        our energy drained,
      our intentions splintered,
        our love glazed over,
      our hopes unmet,
        our faith frayed.

Still, we gasp to thank you
  for this undeniable impulse
    to thank you,
  for this insistent yearning
    to know you,
  for this throbbing desire
    to love you back;
  for this quick, trembling,
    sensuous sense of all your gifts
      showered like rain on lives
        long parched by inattention:
  bread to empower our bodies,
    beauty to quicken our pulse,
      night to show off the stars
        and put us in our awesome place,

problems to summon our talents,
  love to link our lives,
    laughter to nurse our wounds,
passion to shape our maybes
  into a brighter day for
    the whole human family;
and for this mystical, magical moment
  of peace and shimmering power,
    of grace and prophetic stretch,
in which you work the miracles
  of gladdening our hearts yet again,
    in spite of painful patches,
      sobering losses, and puzzling trials;
  of balming our souls with a touch of joy
    because we are,
      and are yours,
        and you are forever;
  of heeding our prayers beyond our words
    in the spirit of Jesus. Amen.

Breathe Deeply into Us

Worn into a Hallowed Glow

Gratitude comes hard to us, God.
    Boasting and blaming are easier,
        yet we trust you know
            those are symptoms of the insecurities,
                terrors, and ambitions that drive us
                      to anxious distractions and duplicities.

But now, in your presence,
    in this place, with this beloved company,
        we are softened into clarity and praise,
            into awareness of our too-pinched lives
                and your expansive grace.

    So on this day fringed with blessed memories
        and woven with amazing possibilities,
            we contritely pause to praise you
                for the way our lives are braided together
                      to sustain and enrich each one of us
                          beyond our ready notice,
                      and to give us chances, day by day,
                        beyond our ready risking
                            were we not alerted and encouraged
                              by the imagination and compassion
                                of all of us held together in your embrace.

We praise you for this church's
    oh-so-human witness to the holy mystery
        of Jesus' life and death and resurrection,
    for the halting yet certain way
        we have been worn into a hallowed glow
            by our prayers and tears,
                songs and laughter,
                    celebrations and sorrows,
                        disputes and reconciliations,
    and for our fitful struggle to strive first
        for your kingdom, by your power,
            to your glory, through your mercy.

We praise you that when we gather in your name,
        you are in our midst to disturb and renew us;
    that when we risk some smidgen for justice,
        you multiply the loaves and fishes of our deeds;
    that when we seek the demanding way of peace,
        we are found by a peace, a hope, an empowerment
            that the world cannot give or take away.

In that peace and power
    we take hopeful heart,
        walk on without fainting,
            and confidently pray. Amen.

Worn into a Hallowed Glow

We Dare to Speak Your Name

O God,
    we dare to speak your name
        at threat of having our mouths stopped,
    for your name is holy,
        and wherever we are
            we ought take off our shoes,
                for all ground everywhere is sacred.

Still, we pray in your presence here
    that our spirits be joyous,
        our words be inspired and true,
           our works hereafter be just.

Renew our minds and bodies
    to be fresh and vital as morning light,
        and grant us peace within
           deep as the starry night.

Open our eyes to your glory
    in the subtle dazzle of everything,
        in the lives of every living thing,
           that everywhere and at all times
                we assuredly be mindful of you.

Deliver us from captivity
    to comfort and security and propriety
        that we may be free to risk for you
           at every turn and circumstance.

We Dare to Speak Your Name

Make us brave and bold and scrupled enough
   to know that to love our enemies
      does not mean to be afraid to make them
         in a daily thrust toward justice
         and in the bold venture
            of saying what we mean,
               and meaning what we say,
         in a trustworthy strive toward intimacy.

Awaken us to the task of becoming beautiful
   in spirit, mind and heart, and so in face,
      that our gifts be worthy of your grace.

Arouse us to pay the price of being merciful
   that our lives reflect your mercy to us.

Empower us to dare
   to be compassionate
      that your dreams for our humanity come true,
   to be imaginative
      that your kingdom come in and through us,
   to be disciplined yet flexible
      that we may prepare the way for you
         in our hearts and in your world;
            through Jesus Christ our Lord. Amen.

We Dare to Speak Your Name

Hover Over Us

God of passionate patience
   and lively waiting,
      in whatever way you choose,
  be with us in our eagerness
    and in our uneasiness
as we balance on the edge
   of a newness disguised as familiar,
     a mystery lurking in the taken-for-granted,
       a discovery waiting in the common,
        a love fevering to be expressed,
          a hope waiting to be born out of pain,
  and the wonder of it all as it hushes our hearts
    and disquiets our certainties.

God, without you
  we are truly scared stiff
    of making mistakes,
      of being ridiculed
        or rejected
          or missing out
  in our always fumbling uncertainties.

So we pray that your Spirit
  will hover over us to enable us
    to separate, with you,
      the light from the darkness
        in the change that seeks to shape us,
          and which we seek creatively to shape.

Hover Over Us

We pray that your Spirit lift us
   and encourage us to keep getting up
      and going on,
         no matter how many times
            we have tripped up and fallen crying down.

We pray that your Spirit empower us
   to crack the smothering crust of deadening habits
      and goad us to set out after fresh dreams.

We pray that your Spirit liberate and lead us
   in laboring for healing for the broken,
      justice for the exploited,
         chances for the oppressed,
            peace for the violated and the violent of the earth.

So move in and among us
   that we may grow in your Spirit,
      rejoice in your kingdom,
         and live with passion
            this amazing life that, by your grace,
               is in us and that we are gratefully in. Amen.

Hover Over Us

Prayers OF PRAISE

The Weave of Miracles

Praise be to you, gracious God,
    for this day, this earth, this life,
        for the weave of miracles blessing us
            and for your quiet power sustaining us.

We praise you for times of laughter and tears,
    risk and reconciliation,
        reflection and healing,
    and for the stubborn presence of your Spirit
        making it all sacred.

Praise be to you, awesome God,
    for the holy mysteries
        of our struggling and wondering,
    for our trials and triumphs,
        and all that moves us to awe,
            to love, to pray, to serve,
    since it is your Spirit that moves us so
        and is creating us still;
    through our Lord Jesus Christ. Amen.

The Surprises of Grace

Holy One, we stammer to you
   our praise and thanksgiving
      for the extravagance of gifts
   that often leave us tongue-tied
      and teary-eyed,
   yet with gladness of heart,
      quietness of mind,
         and lightness of spirit.

We thank you not only for our days
   but for what you fill them with:
      the spray of light,
         the play of seasons,
            the labors of love,
      the reach toward justice,
         the embrace of beauty,
            the tinge of glory.

Wondrous One, we praise you
   for the surprises of grace
      that catch us off guard
and fill our silences with ease,
      our struggles with hope,
         our friendships with power,
      our defeats with timeless lessons
         and with the fresh possibilities
            that well up from the old promises
               you always find new ways to keep;
through Christ Jesus our Lord. Amen.

Wonders that Seize Our Hearts

O God of awesome holiness,
    in this quick, glad now
        praise surges in us.
We seek words to carry to you
    the wonders that seize our hearts.

Praise be to you for raising us
    to live in this vibrant time,
        on this nurturing earth,
            with these caring friends
    as warriors of compassion,
        witnesses to justice,
            revelers in joy.

We rejoice to be alive!
    We rejoice in your presence!
We rejoice for the healing of wounds,
    the stirring of dreams,
        the surging of strengths,
    the gushing of laughter,
        the cleansing of tears,
            the easing of shame,
    the singing of songs,
        the deepening of silence,
            the urging of stars.

So we rejoice that the rhythms of our lives
    mysteriously catch the cadences of your grace
        and, again and again, forever,
            we are raised by you to life with you;
                through Christ our Lord.
                Amen.

Wonders that Seize Our Hearts

One Moment of Praise

O God of every now, and then,
> we pause for one moment to praise you
>> for all the moments of our lives.

We praise you for the glorious moments:
> bread, the intimacy of lovers, lilacs, morning coffee,
>> a rooted word, a rapturous song, a circle of stories,
>>> the scrunch of oldsters at play, children at prayer.

We praise you for the shared moments:
> honest exchange, deepening trust, earned friendship,
>> smudgy work, a ballet of ideas, a lullaby of quietness,
>>> trouble met, the release of tears, the easing of fears,
>>>> the renewing of wonder, the embracing of mystery.

We praise you for the surprising moments:
> the wink of a stranger, the flutter of hope in the stillness,
>> the enchantment of a rainbow and claim of a promise kept,
>>> the goodness beneath the flurry of things,
>>>> beauty out of the muck,
>>>>> the clarified direction in a prayer,
>>>>>> a light in the soul's night.

We praise you for the holy moments:
> all the bearers of love, of truth, of mercy,
>> of meaning, of demand, of amazement,
> all that nudges us to readiness for the risks of faith,
>> the mysterious all that attaches us to your grace
>>> from which nothing can separate us.

O God, we praise you for every moment,
> for you, source of each moment,
>> and present in all moments, always, in all ways.
>>> Amen.

One Moment of Praise

In the Silence Between Our Heartbeats

God of this sacramental planet,
   poet of the language this universe speaks,
      resident not only of the out-there for all of us,
         but the in-here of each of us,
  where can we be where you are not?
    Who can we be with whom you are not?

From the depths of our yearning
   in which you stir and summon us,
      we scramble for words prodigious enough
         to carry the awe, the gratitude, the sensual delight,
            the tingly praise of our hearts and skin, eyes and ears,
               for gifts our minds already know far outnumber
                  all the trips those words could ever make.

We rejoice in this season of soft-slanted sunlight
   for throat-lumping pirouettes of scarlet, orange, and gold
      twirled up toward a reach of cloud-scrubbed skies
         or floated down to a waiting catch of brown and green;
  for this season of stunning, steady ripening and readying of things
      against the lowering of longer, cooler nights.

We rejoice for what is ripening and readying within and among us,
   for selves and lives worth the hard hallowing and claiming,
      for relationships worth the continuous and rewarding struggle,
         for shafts of light spilling in our souls,
            for humor, hope, and courage,
               for compassion and mercy
                  and commitment to justice and peace.

In the Silence Between Our Heartbeats

O Holy One,
    in and through the many of us,
        in and beyond the all of everything,
            in and under the truth between the lines of each of our lives,
    heed the hundred prayers
        scuffling under this spoken one.

Hear what our hearts ache to whisper, sing, scream to you,
    then let it echo in us until we hear your answer in it,
        until we sense that it is your presence
            that touches and terrifies and fascinates us,
    that signals us, in the silence between our heartbeats,
        to move on with you to depths beneath the familiar,
            truer than the comfortable, more exciting than certainty.

Enable us, by your grace and empowerment,
    to become expanders of life,
        scatterers of laughter,
            singers of songs,
                makers of peace,
    spreaders of good news,
        healers of wounds,
            tellers of truth,
    practitioners of mercy,
        sharers of joy,
            weavers of community,
    walkers in humility,
        fulfillers of your dreams for us
            spun in Jesus, our brother and Lord.
                Amen.

In the Silence Between Our Heartbeats

The Deepest Wonder of All

O God of imponderable elegance,
    the wonder of it all is that we are here at all,
        in this specific place and time,
            living these distinctive lives
                on this singular planet.

The wonder is that we are not lost in the stars,
    that you move in such diverse ways to claim us,
        making loves as mysteriously real as galaxies,
            challenging us with friends and adversaries,
    stirring us to stories, music, and prayers
        that bind us to the whirling heavens,
            the fascinating present, charged future,
                and spirited earthiness of each other.

The wonder is that your Spirit moves
    over the welter of our lives
        so light slivers the darkness,
            old fears and prejudices crumble,
                mercy keeps turning us loose
    to transform anguish into wisdom, pain into beauty,
        failure into freedom, guilt into understanding,
            until your kingdom comes a sigh or two closer.

The wonder is that there are those among us
    compassionate enough to stand against cruelty,
        fierce enough to be an antidote against indifference,
    courageous enough to hold power accountable,
        prophetic enough to expose the poverty of wealth,
    unflinching enough to stare down violence,
        compelling enough for us to join them.

O God, the wonder is that you are the deepest wonder of all.
   So we pray, in the wonder of expectation,
      that you deepen us into such amazement
         as will derange us into joy,
            and rearrange us into bolder witnesses to your kingdom
               and more trustworthy members of your church,
                  which has become too often piously distracted
                     by its wrinkled certainties,
                  blindly proud of its withering strengths,
                     proudly blind to its foibles and weaknesses,
   that we be pried open and eager
      for the surprises and chances
         you ingeniously visit upon us.

O God, the wonder is that in Jesus you show us
   that a love affair with us is what you want most deeply,
      and a love affair with you is what we want most truly,
a love affair with you, and so with neighbor and enemy and self,
   because we are yours and they are yours,
      and all loving is for our sake, their sake, your sake
         and loving at all is the wonder of us,
            even as all loving is the wonder of you.
         Amen.

The Deepest Wonder of All

Grace Beyond Our Grasp

Holy God, the mystery of your infinite loftiness
   is not greater than that of your imminent presence,
     and we gather in awe of both and of you.

In this moment we thank you for lacing
   eternity into our time,
      the longing for what lasts into our hearts,
         traces of your kingdom into the round of our days,
            the assurance that you have made us for yourself
               into core of our souls.

We praise you for the joy that renews us
   through the miracle of each other,
     the wonder of children,
       the sharing of bread,
         the occasions of justice,
     the healing of music,
       the sprawl of sunsets,
         the scatter of stars,
     the anchoring of prayer,
       the gift of Christ,
         the summons of your Spirit
   making us small but blest partners
     in your ongoing creation.

For your grace beyond our grasp,
   we praise you and ask
     that you deepen our faith
       and strengthen our faithfulness;
         through Jesus Christ our Lord.
           Amen.

Grace Beyond Our Grasp

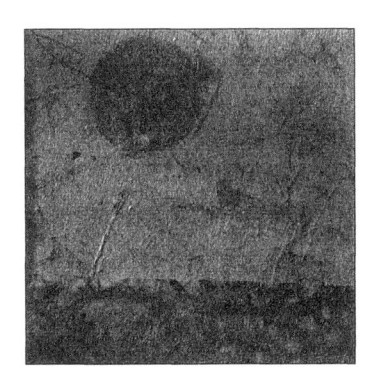

Prayers OF THANKSGIVING

Beautiful Beyond All Telling

For this wondrous world you created,
   and are creating still,
      mountains and seas, lands and peoples
         beautiful beyond all telling of it,
            we thank you, O God of us all.

For the common humanity
   you created us to be,
      one family joined in the mystery of you,
         yet babbled into many branches
            to challenge and enrich us all,
               and deliver any from arrogant over-reach,
                  we thank you, O God of mercy and wisdom.

For the laughter and wonder and wisdom,
   the longing and caring and trusting
      that link us at our core,
         and shape our shared future,
            beautiful beyond all telling of it,
               we thank you, O Father/Mother of us all.

For your insistent call
   to hallow our lives by loving
      our neighbors as ourselves,
         our enemies as our neighbors,
            and you above all,
   we would thank you
      with our lives as well as our lips,
         for only so will we become

       doers of your will,
           fulfillers of your dream,
               members in truth of your human family,
                   and beautiful beyond all telling of it,
                     O Judge and Lover of us all.

For your promise to be with us always,
   to disturb our consciences,
      ignite our curiosity,
         gladden our hearts,
  compose our wills,
     deepen our relationships,
        rouse your image in us,
           we thank you for shaping our lives
               to become beautiful beyond all telling of it,
                  O God of faithfulness and ingenuity.

For your claiming our lives
   to serve your kingdom of justice and peace
      and to share its joy
         in redeeming the soul of our time,
     as we join to help your human family
        become beautiful beyond all telling of it,
           we thank you, O God of power and glory;
               through Jesus Christ, our brother and Lord.
            Amen.

Beautiful Beyond All Telling

Thankful Beyond Understanding

O God, source of this whole shebang,
    we thank you that in your bewildering wisdom,
        and for your oft puzzling purposes,
    you launched us on this wondrous exodus of life
        toward the promised time of freedom and fulfillment,
    and that in your staggering compassion
        you girded up to be our traveling companion
            until we find our way to each other
                and your kingdom.

We are thankful to you
    for gifts of taken-for-granted commonness:
        the song of a bird, the strum of wind, a hundred shades of green,
            a parent's praying patience, a friend's voice, a changed way,
                work worth doing, children's questions, a new thought;
        our bodies, enough food, wine slowly shared, a quiet walk,
            the touch of hands, catch of eyes, hark of dreams,
                the wash of rain, snuggle of darkness, stardust on the roof,
    the assuring, disquieting sense of your presence in it all,
        the goad to repentance, the nudge to gratitude
            in the utterly everywhere of small miracles.

Most of all we are thankful beyond understanding it
    that even in adversity, pain, and suffering,
        even in the face of defeat and death, as in all else,
            your Spirit labors for our healing, resilience, and deliverance,
                leaving on us your eternal fingerprints of grace and glory;
                through Christ our Lord.
                Amen.

There Is Yet Love

O God of stunning surprises and uncanny support,
   your foolishness is our hope,
      your lavishness our sustenance,
         your toughness our encouragement,
            your gentleness our ease and re-creation,
               your gifts within gifts within gifts our awe and joy.

Even as we pray, deepen us in the ways of gratitude,
   of alertness, awareness, imagination, discernment,
not to celebrate fantasies
   but to see what is profoundly real:
      blessings so close and constant
         we scarcely notice or name them as such.
Now before you, with you, we would so see and thank you.

There is yet beauty in this strident, scarred world,
   for we have heard strains of it, seen splashes of it,
      felt the shock and power, draw and renewal of it,
         and been quickened for a time,
            even jolted to add a jot and whit
               to creating a new, brighter world.
We thank you and ask for keener ears,
   sharper eyes, bolder minds, stronger voices.

There is yet love in this violent world,
   for we have experienced it undeservedly,
      even risked it in moments that claimed us,
         and been changed by it little by little.
We thank you for it and ask for larger hearts,
   wider reach, more daring spirits, more permeable time,
      more generous intentions, more inclusive communities.

There Is Yet Love

There is yet justice in this greedy, get-over world,
   for we have witnessed it, watched its ripples,
     and been humbled and heartened,
        even drawn to add the ounces of our weight
          to tip the scale toward it sometimes.
  We thank you for it, and ask for less caution,
    less calculation and resistance to its summons,
      and so to count ourselves among those happy ones
        blest to rise to its challenge in our time and place,
          for there is nothing trivial
            about this gift of life you share with us, God,
              nor frivolous in this creating you are about.

There is yet the whirl of stars and atoms,
   the light of the sun, the climb of green toward it,
    the stretch of our souls toward it,
      the delight of children in it,
        the healing, and wonder of it,
  and the web and nurture
    of the friendship it generates,
      for we have been awed by it all,
        endowed with it all,
          and given the chance to hallow it all,
          and we thank you.

So we thank you the more
  for those who are the hallowers,
    who show us what it means
      to see and make all things holy:
  the fidelity of those who rise each day
    to care for the children, watch over the sick,
      and do the thousand thankless tasks
        that sustain us and the community;

There Is Yet Love

for the courage and honesty of poets and prophets
    whose words and images and visions
        take us into your presence;
for all who say what they mean
    and mean what they say,
        and build trust among us;
for all those whose gifts and claims
    make our days like a string of pearls of great price,
        and loosen in us now our tumbling gratitude;
for all the constantly compassionate ways
    you care for us, and share with us,
        the mysterious power and insistent will
            to build, to sing, to heal, to speak,
                to listen, to strive for peace,
            to walk the narrow way between
                justice and mercy toward full humanity,
            to be faithful, bold, quiet of heart,
                and to pray as people created for,
                      and summoned by, joy.
    There is nothing else to say
        except thank you and Amen.

There Is Yet Love

Transform Our Gratitude into Courage

O God, we are in awe of your grace,
   tough enough to withstand
      the tantrums of our arrogance
         and the snubs of our indifference,
   tender enough to sometimes soften
      our on-guard hearts into humility,
         our criticisms into compassion,
creative enough to raise up
      in every generation and in our midst witnesses
         to take up the torch of your passion and purposes,
            to speak your word in a new language,
         to lead this human family of yours, and ours,
            on our common exodus to justice
               and toward a peaceable kingdom and joy.

How shall we express our gratitude to you
      except by girding up to follow those witnesses.
Strengthen us to walk and work, pray and speak,
   to confront the furies of hate and fear,
      to overthrow the barriers of discrimination,
   to repair the breach of oppression and exploitation
      in the body of our single humanity,
   to join in the witness to integrity and boldness
      that makes bright the time of our lives.

We pray not in despair, O Lord, but in thanksgiving
   that justice still insists its way into our oft resistant world,
      that it continues to be made flesh in the lives
         of nameless people whose clarity of vision,
            concerns of spirit, and commitments of conscience
               enrich our common life in untold but unfailing ways.

We would gratefully lift those witnesses up to you now
    and honor them before you who know them as we do not,
        for you reside not only with the least of those in need,
            but with those least in vanity or acclaim,
                who know what it is to walk humbly with you.

O God of such holiness
    as disturbs all easy contentment,
        all frivolous self-seeking,
            all idolatrous claims of privilege,
    by your grace jolt and transform our gratitude
        into the courage to risk security for justice,
            that we and the human family
                no longer continue to unravel
                    into the frivolity and hollowness
                        of merely personal and private pursuits
                            that corrode the bonds of community.

Make us bold and visionary enough
    to measure our lives not so much
        by victories won or successes achieved
    but by worthy battles engaged,
        scars of faith endured,
            noble comrades joined.

Help us to learn by heart
        the lessons of love you bear on your heart,
    until we wrestle from the depths of our souls
        the ways of love,
            the perspectives of laughter,
                the proportions of your eternal kingdom
                    that make precious our limited time,

Transform Our Gratitude into Courage

so we will keep our balance
> amidst the hucksters of this world
and take you more seriously
> than we take ourselves
because you take us more seriously
> than eye has seen or ear heard
> > or imagination reached.

So, God of this ongoing exodus,
> we shall sing our thanksgiving to you
> > as we follow you day by night by day,
> out of our addiction to the lesser goods and gods
> > of our own biases, certainties, and dreams
> toward the vast forever spaces and relationships
> > of your dream for us of a kingdom
> > > where we listen to and respect each other,
> > > > appreciate and learn from each other,
> > > where no one's need is ignored,
> > > > no one's gift turned away,
> > > where we are as generous with each other
> > > > and the whole family of creation,
> > > > > as you are with us,
> > > and we are as truly free,
> > > > as firmly bound,
> > > > > as deeply grateful,
> > > > > > as everlastingly joyful,
> > > as you mean us to be;
> > > > in the spirit of Jesus.
> > > > > Amen.

Transform Our Gratitude into Courage

Prayers OF CONFESSION

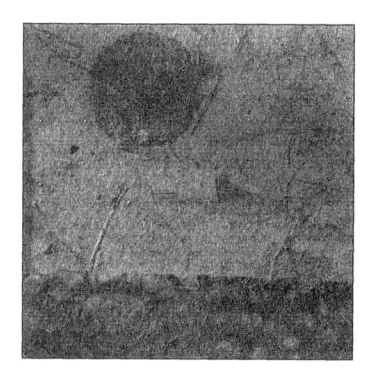

Deepen Our Longing into Trust

From beneath the clutter of our lives,
    we call out to you, O God.
It is not so much that we have chosen evil
    as that we have pursued little goods
        and lesser gods,
            until we have lost our way.

Our love has become too narrow,
    our excuses too wide,
        our blaming too quick
            our forgiveness too slow,
                our gratitude too rare.

Forgive us!
    By your mercy, deepen our longing into trust,
        our pride into compassion,
            our fear into courage,
                our frustration into creativity,
                    our timidity into boldness,
                        our prayers into actions,
                            however small and simple.

Then by your sneaky power,
    multiply the loaves and fishes of those actions
        into food enough for a small, simple portion
            for each one of your magnificent, needy multitude
                of the precious, companion bumblers
                    you have lead with us to this day
                        and are guiding home to your kingdom;
                      through Christ our Lord.
                    Amen.

Let the Healing Begin

O Father-Mother of us all, we gather as those blest
    that you temper judgment with patience,
        else we could not gather at all.
So we bring to you
    not only our bungling and betrayals
        but those we have wounded
            by our faithlessness and indifference.
We bring to you those we love
    but less fully than we would
        were we not so defensive
            or so easily frightened by intimacy.
We bring to you those with whom we work
    but less well than we would
        were we not so obsessed with power
            or so arrogantly ready to judge.
We bring to you those we live with in this society
    but less closely than we would
        were we not so fearfully suspicious
            or so insistent on measuring them
                by our comfortable biases and certainties.
O God, by your mercy, heal the wounds
    we have inflicted on others and ourselves.
Let that healing begin with us
    in the knowledge that with mercy
        comes the power and pressure to risk
            the honesty and humility that will move us
                toward wholeness within each and among all
        through reclaiming and rejoicing in our common humanity,
            as your still beloved family;
                through our brother and Lord, Jesus Christ. Amen.

Let the Healing Begin

Come Now to Find Us

O God of such truth as sweeps away all lies,
    of such grace as shrivels all excuses,
  come now to find us
      for we have lost our selves
        in a shuffle of disguises
          and the rattle of empty words.

Let your Spirit move mercifully
    to recreate us from
      the chaos of our lives.

We have been careless
    of our days,
      our loves,
        our gifts,
          our chances.

We withdraw in arrogance,
    hide in timidity,
      disappear in fear
        rather than reaching out in hope,
          engaging in humility,
            risking in faith.

We are busy in self-seeking,
    lax in self-awareness.

We seek the comfort of belonging,
    shun the cost of responsibility.

Come Now to Find Us

We are long on easy generalities,
   short on hard specifics.

Our prayer is to change, O God,
   not out of despair of self
      but for love of you,
         and for the selves we long to become
            before we simply waste away.

Let your mercy move in and through us now,
   freeing us to love honestly,
      enabling us to trust bravely,
         reuniting us to live joyfully,
            and claiming us for the audacious revolution
               of Christ and your kingdom.
                 Amen.

Come Now to Find Us

You Know the Secrets

Holy God,
    you know the secrets in which we hide
        and from which we hide.
    So it is the sense of your judgment,
        the awareness of your aching disappointment,
            the haunt of your merciful healing
                that move us to seek with you
                      the truth that will set us free.

Lord, you know the truth is that too often
    we give in to the temptations
        to live to please ourselves and others
            rather than to please you,
        to seek for ourselves
            status, achievements, and acclaim
                that belong only to you.

Lord, you know the truth is that too often
    we excuse ourselves by claiming
        that we know too much, or too little,
            to trust you or seek your will,
        that we are so good and right
            we must insist on our own way,
    or that we are so flawed
        we must use self-pity to control others,
    that we are too sensitive and humble
        to be honest with others or ourselves.

Lord, you know the truth is that too often
    we are harsh, indifferent, weary, scared, and greedy,
        retributive, merciless, dishonest, envious, and blaming,
    removed from our own heart and your image in us,
        distant from tenderness, faithfulness, and joy.

Yet, Lord, you know, as we too often forget,
    that the greatest truth of all,
        and by your grace, the greatest truth of us,
            is that even now, as always,
                we are never far from your heart,
                      or at remove from your mercy.

So we fervently ask you to soften us,
    to forgive and heal us of our fretful fears,
        to restore us to our truest selves,
    to reconcile us to each other
        and to you, Mother-Father of us all.

Then in the freedom of your truth for us,
    we would set out with you once more
        for your kingdom of justice, peace,
            and such jubilation as eye has not yet seen,
            nor ear heard,
            nor heart known,
yet that is what you promise
    and purpose for us there,
        but still scatter in a multitude of moments
            for us to attend to here along our way,
                even as you gathered them once, and still,
                    in the life of Jesus Christ our Lord.
                    Amen.

You Know the Secrets

Restore Our Souls to Singing

Please, do not weary of us, O God,
    as yet again we open before you
        the dark places of our lives
            and seek the healing of your light.

Forgive us for the pace
    that forgets you and snarls our days
        in a faithless scramble
            to make more ends meet
                than we can manage
                      or than you purpose for us.

Lord, we lose the piping of your kingdom
    in trumpeting desires that mislead
        and leave us vexed by disappointments
            that make us bitter,
    in booming angers that make us lash out,
        and lash in, destructively,
    in shrieking fears that deafen us
        and scapegoat those who are different,
    in whining cynicism that turns us
        to jaded pursuits and mocking nightmares,
    in strumming arrogance that twists us
        away from our own and each other's face and truth
            and muffles the cry of our deep need for you.

So do we corrode love,
>   bruise those closest to us,
>   turn cowardly at the summons of justice,
>   slow leak our lives of hope and joy,
>   fray the ties of community,
>   forsake the peace the world cannot give
>   for the loneliness, anxiety, and emptiness it can.

O Physician of our souls,
>   heal us of our self-inflicted wounds
>   and the several dis-eases others
>   have thoughtlessly bequeathed us,
>   and we them,
>   and use us as your instruments
>   in healing those we have wounded.

Mercy us into humility and gratitude,
>   restore our souls to singing,
>   our hearts to loving,
>   our hands to doing justice.

Empower us to press on still and sturdily
>   in the way you have shown us in Christ
>   until we know in our blood and bones
>   that nothing can separate us from your love.
>   Amen.

Restore Our Souls to Singing

Restore the Circle of Humanity

Holy God,
    judge us as only you can,
        with scouring truth
            and rinsing encouragement,
    for, left to ourselves,
        we are anxiously condemning
            or angrily defensive.

By your mercy
    restore the circle of humanity
        we have broken
    by our acts and attitudes
        of exclusion and indifference,
    our homophobia and faithless biases,
        our mindless competitiveness,
    our niceness at the cost of honesty,
        our pretenses that distance us,
    our fear of guileless intimacy,
        our hypocrisy in blaming and ignoring
            the victims of injustice,
    our timid collusion in the unraveling
        of community and the spiraling down
            of our common society into the pursuit
                of merely personal, private, even pious goals.

God of our noblest dreams and deepest hopes,
   restore in us clean hearts,
      right minds, a glad resolve
         to help remold the soul of our time,
            to rejoin the private lives of each of us
               to the public life of all of us
                  and the promise of your kingdom.

By your canny power,
   pressure us not to compromise our integrity into duplicity,
      our passion into passivity,
         our creativity into conformity,
            our compassion into indifference,
               our conscience into cynicism,
   that we neither betray
      the deepest longing of our humanity
         for the bondage of seductive false security,
   nor forsake the audacity of our faith
      for the conformity of juiceless trivial pursuits.

So, by your grace, shall we be mercifully set free
   to join with you in healing the broken heart
      and broken circle of your human family,
         and find our lives stretched to joyful proportions
            by the stunning grace of Jesus Christ our Lord.
               Amen.

Restore the Circle of Humanity

Home at Last

O Gracious God,
    whose lover's quarrel with us
        is our anguish, history, and hope,
    we confess that too often we lack courage
        to join your lover's quarrel
            with ourselves and the world.
We have not quarreled with power
    when it's used only for the privilege of a few
        because too often we're the privileged.
We have not quarreled with the cleverness
    that twists truth into lies to profit some
        because too often we've profited.
We have not quarreled with the arrogance
    that dictates the dominance of one race,
        or nation, or gender, or religion
            because too often we're the dominant.
Have mercy on us, heal us, Lord,
    and deliver us from our self-promotion,
        cowardice, and lack of compassion.
Then empower us to be among those
    who dare to do the things that are just and beautiful,
        true and faithful, visionary and deeply joyful,
    so we may be free and whole
        and home at last, home where we belong,
            home with our true selves,
                home with each other,
                    home in the human family,
                      home with you;
                          through Christ our Lord.
                          Amen.

Home at Last

Prayers
OF PETITION

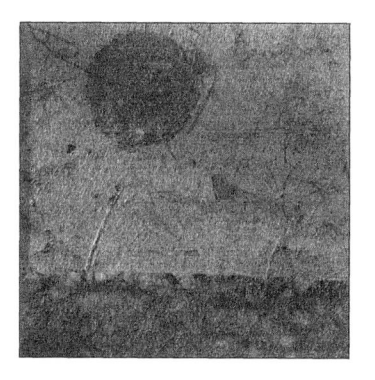

Listen to the Longing

Lord, we have only human words
    to address you lest we be
        entirely dumb before you.

So, listen now, beneath our words,
    to the longing that reaches toward you
        and the gratitude that beats in our hearts
            and fills us with joy for everything
                that is just and true, good and human,
        all the gritty, muddy, bony, bloody, hairy,
            sweaty, smelly, beautiful, tough, tender,
                possibility-laced, throbbing living-ness of it.

Forgive us for taking it all for granted,
    for acting as though it is not a gift but ours by right,
        as though there is not enough for everyone;
    for hunkering down in our race or nationality,
        our gender or class or culture or religious dogma,
            our sexual orientation, or political one,
                assuming they stake the boundaries of your kingdom.

Scorch into our souls once more the awesome truth
    that you have entrusted us with the great, glad responsibility
        of handing on abundant life to our children
            and our children's children.

Excite your image in us
> that we may sweat and pray, sing and battle,
>> sacrifice and rejoice, be eager yet at ease
>>> in the task of giving them bread, not stones,
> and leaving them not violence or any kind of poverty,
>> but freedom, a treasure of chances,
>>> green forests, sparkling seas, scoured air,
>>>> and a legacy of compassion and peace
because in our time we have walked together with you,
> as sisters and brothers in the human family,
>> and shared mercy and lived bravely and faithfully,
>>> justly, and thankfully as followers of Jesus.
>>> Amen.

Listen to the Longing

Let Your Kingdom Be the North Star for Us

Inescapable God,
    Lover more intimate than our secret thoughts,
        than the rhythm of our hearts,
            the rise and fall of our breathing,
                the music of our longing,
                      the haunt of our conscience,
    we blush in your presence
        because you know us altogether.

Our sin is not hid from you,
    busy as we are in our shell game
        of disguise and denial and self-exaggeration.
Yet in moments of utter honesty, such as this,
    neither is it wholly hid from us.
So we do not pray to tell you of it,
    or wallow in it, or use it as an occasion for pious sentiment,
        or make it an excuse for avoiding the fray,
            or counter it with our not-trivial achievements,
    but to remind ourselves that our truest hope
        and surest ease is in your power and not our own.

O gracious God,
    out of the throb of our poverty and fear,
        the restless ache of unused, misused talents,
            the breathless pursuit of what does not satisfy,
                and the curdle of love become timid,
we turn to you, trusting that you not only know
    our frailties and failures and inflated successes,
        but that you know them in cleansing judgment,
            tender mercy, and begin-again healing.

Deepen us in patience
   and stretch our capacity to laugh
      when we take ourselves more seriously
         than we take you.

Renew now our vision
   of who you created us to be,
      and what you call us to do,
   of wild goodness and disruptive faithfulness,
      of cheeky risks for justice,
   of hearty inclusion of the rejected,
      of death-defying insistence that there are enough
         riches of bread, of things and truth and beauty,
            more than enough of the riches of grace and you
               for us all to gladly share and live in peace.

Let your kingdom be the North Star for us
   in our dogged exodus from addiction to fear and falsehood
      to the wholeness of that life together and with you
         for which we so fiercely long
            and for which you so fervently create us,
               even now, even all of us.
                  Amen.

Let Your Kingdom Be the North Star for Us

Strengthen Us to Answer with Brave Hearts

God of grace,
    as you did with *{Rosa Parks and Martin Luther King, Jr.,*
        Mother Teresa, Nelson Mandela, and Desmond Tutu},*
        strengthen us to answer with brave hearts
            your call to help shape a world
                not of death and oppression
                    but of life and hope.

God of power, strengthen us to help shape a country
    where our children will be free of the burdens
        of racism and sexism, fear and exploitation,
            violence and indifference, greed and pollution;
    where all people work with dignity,
        are rewarded fairly, and respected fully;
    where labor, rest, play, and worship
        are in blessed, graceful balance.

God of glory, strengthen us to help shape a society
    where the value of families is reflected
        in decent homes, good schools,
            safe neighborhoods, mutually earned trust
                glad gatherings, respected differences;
    where older persons are not forgotten,
        trivialized, marginalized or brutalized,
            but honored for their experience,
                cherished for their gifts,
                    sought for their wisdom.

* *Insert names of your choice.*

Strengthen Us to Answer with Brave Hearts

God of mercy, strengthen us to help shape a nation
 where diversity is a source of enrichment,
  compassion is common, life's poetry realized,
   suffering lightened through sharing,
    justice attended, joy pervasive, hope lived,
     the hum of the universe heard,
 and together with you and with each other
  we build what is beautiful, true,
   and worthy of your generosity to us,
    an echo of your kingdom.

With the passion of the prophets,
 and in the insistent spirit of Jesus,
  we say, Amen and Amen.

Strengthen Us to Answer with Brave Hearts

Go Deeper, Further With Us

God of ordinary things like bread and wine,
    and ordinary people like all of us,
  we remember in exacting gratitude
    that though our reach is far too short
      to touch with healing and with help
        all the ache and need of your human family,
          or even of each other here,
  our reach is not too short
    to give of ourselves,
      our time and heart and hand—
  give not just what we wish or want or feel,
    but, in faithful honesty, give everything we can;
  nor is our reach too short
    to lift all of us to you
      for hope and peace and strength, as now we do.

We pray fervently
  for those we love deeply
    but painfully disappoint and cruelly diminish
      by taking them carelessly for granted;
  for those, out of our peevish busy-ness,
    we love too little, pilfering their preciousness;
  for those, in our tight heartedness, we love poorly
    and so impoverish terribly, along with ourselves.

Go deeper, further with us, Lord,
  off our timid, sheltered way
    into a generous, daring craziness,
  so we may learn what it means
    to love our neighbor as our self
      and you above all,

and so become free and faithful enough
> to sift the substance of what matters
>> from the gruel of the perishable,
and come to know the power of prayer
> that drives us from our knees
>> into the fray of your answers.

So we pray now for the poor, the sick, the misbegotten,
> the oppressed, exploited, marginalized, forgotten.
Be with them in your healing power
> and lay them on our consciences and hearts,
>> and on those of our nation's leaders,
that callousness not lead to insane holocausts
> but to the reach of common humanity
>> toward justice, welcoming inclusion,
>>> an awesome respect for our human ecosystem,
>>>> and our proper place in your scheme of things.

O God, shred the foolish finery of our arrogance
> and from its scraps mercifully stitch
>> robes of enough-for-all compassion
>>> for us to throw around those close in our families,
>>>> and in our neighborhoods and city,
>>> our nation and our world
>>>> who shiver in desperate need,
>>> and around ourselves as well,
>>>> and the soul-deep need that makes us shiver, too.

For all our sisters and brothers, and for ourselves,
> we pray, trusting the sneakiness of your answers
>> and praising you for your boundless mercy
>>> from which all new chances come,
>>>> through Jesus our first brother and our Lord.
>>>>> Amen.

Go Deeper, Further With Us

We Dare to Ask

O God of limitless embrace
    of every time, then and now and not yet,
        of all light years of space
            and all darkness in between,
    of the covenant with each living creature
        back there once, and here today and still to be,
you seem too big to pray to sometimes,
    the whole world too much to pray for,
        all our prayers too poor to matter but a mite
            in so vast a concern as must be yours.

Still it is the gift of our smallness that stirs our prayers,
    as well as the grandness of the dreams you put in us,
        the deep need past all filling on our own,
            the anxiety past all stilling by ourselves,
the dauntless gratitude for being part
    of so wondrous an enterprise as life is,
and for the haunt of a dim awareness
    that you want and heed our prayers.
So, great and gracious God,
    we dare to ask these things of you.

For this too-much world
    we know not what to pray except to ask for
        peace in it
            and justice for its people;
        compassion and generosity among as many
            as will risk their private pursuits of the few
                to serve the public good of all;

We Dare to Ask

wisdom to discern that larger good,
> gladness in seeking and serving it;
realization that since we are inescapably connected
> we are also accountable for the beauty and care
>> of this earthly home we share;
courage enough to take the small daily steps
> toward fulfilling your grand dream for us all
>> that in so many ways you share with us
>>> and, in Jesus, show to us.

For ourselves, O God of small things and great sacrifice,
> we ask that in this world
>> where there are at least two sides to anything,
> you would grant us
>> quiet hearts hushed by trusting
>>> that finally all sides of everything are yours,
>> a sense of liberating proportion in the awareness
>>> that therefore all sides are not ours,
>> guidance in choosing daily which side of what
>>> will receive the stubborn ounces of our weight,
>> passion to commit those ounces to tip the scales
>>> toward your kingdom and not to be afraid
>>>> to succeed in full or part or not at all,
>> humility to engage in the human fray
>>> without dehumanizing ourselves
>>> or those who disagree with us,
>> joy in striving to do the much that depends on us
>>> in balance with the ease of confirming
>>>> the infinitely more that depends on you.

And we ask only a few things more, O God,
> a few small, mustard-seed size,
>> faithful, saving things:

We Dare to Ask

to walk with you in each moment
   without plotting for tomorrow,
      and so to really consider the birds of the air,
         the lilies of the field,
            and find the treasures hidden
               in the round of the daily;
to learn by leaning into your Spirit
   to be present to others without preoccupation,
      to engage without having to win,
         to disagree without being judgmental,
to accept outcomes without despair,
   to succeed or fail without misplacing hope,
      to tune to the bracing hum of the stars,
to fathom enough without dismissing fathomless mystery
   of your creation, our brothers and sisters,
      and the grace and mercy and power
         of your embrace that holds close,
            each small one of us,
               and everything all together;
                  in Jesus' name,
                     Amen.

We Dare to Ask

Prayers OF REFLECTION

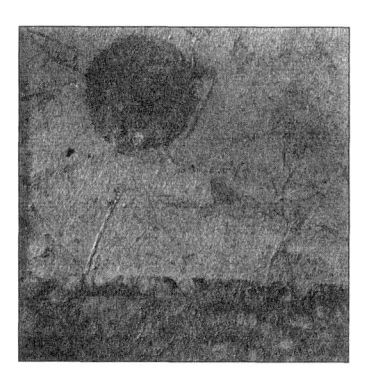

Hold Us in the Embrace of Mercy

O gentle Disturber of the satisfied,
    fierce Comforter of the distressed,
        draw near to welcome us
    as we prodigals return to you
        from the far country of proud negligence
            in rags of longing, need, and sanity.

Hold us for a moment
    in the embrace of mercy and healing,
  that we may learn again and anew
    we are blood-bonded with you;
  that you are gracious far beyond the lesser gods
    of soul-selling popularity and a greed-driven economy,
        of pretentious patriotism, and the community-corroding pursuits
           of private successes and security, careers and causes
              that we have been tunnel-visioned about seeking after
                  and snookered into betting our inheritance on;
  that you are greater still than the legion demons
    of our frantic drivenness and smothering loneliness,
        our nagging doubts and gnawing, twisted-sheets despairs,
           our smirking visitations of guilt,
              our fears of being exposed—
  all the demons that plague and feed us husks
    when we turn from you.

Be with us, stay with us,
    in merrymaking celebration of the mystery
        that you have laced our now with your eternity,
           for we have lost our sense of direction
                in the swirl and glitter of the perishable and trivial.

Hold Us in the Embrace of Mercy

Be with us, stay with us,
> in the ease that comes in the quiet return of attention
>> not only to the small truth in many words
>>> but the great truth in the silence beyond words
>>>> that restores us to some healing proportion
>>>>> and confirms in us the value you confirm on us.

Be with us, stay with us,
> in the urge to imagine ourselves
>> into the wounds and limits, anxieties, needs and burdens
>>> of our most difficult, mirror-image brothers and sisters,
> and to find the humility to blame no more
>> but to reach out to begin with them
>>> the struggle to be reconciled with each other,
>>>> and so with ourselves
>>>>> and with you, the Father-Mother of us all.

Be with us, stay with us,
> through the saving discomfort
>> of our broadest-hearted dream.
> Then confront us with whoever
>> and in whatever wild ways are necessary
>>> to unburden us of our cherished illusions,
>>>> unhinge us from our careful timidities,
>>>>> craze us with glory, with audacity and ecstasy,
>>>>>> and immerse us in such intimacy with you
> as will make something like love and passion,
>> healing and hope happen not only in us but because of us
>>> so we and this world will never be quite the same
>>>> for our being with you here and now, then and there,
>>>>> and you with us wherever and always,
>>>>>> holding us in this amazing love we're forever in;
>> through Jesus the whoever and whatever of it all.   Amen.

Hold Us in the Embrace of Mercy

We Hunger for What You Offer

O God of watchful care,
    night is as day for you,
        and no sparrow falls beyond
            the catch of your eye,
    so you know us all together,
        though our attention to you
            is partial, jumbled, and short.

We gladly gather in this place and time
    set apart for the worship of you,
        while sadly confessing
            that we have been mindless of you
                in most other places and times
                      where we live and work,
                          speak and spend and play.

We have sensed your grace and glory
    in the beauty of the seasons
        but missed it in the people around us,
        the struggles within us,
            the challenges before us.

In the confusion of pride, we have stumbled,
    surrendering to our fears
        more than striving in faith;
    succumbing to the counsels of comfort
        more than rising to the appeals of love
            and the claims of justice;
    cleaving to our impulses for security
        more than our longing for freedom
            and the challenge to use it creatively;

bowing to our addiction to blaming
and the illusion of innocence
more than taking responsibility
and attending to our need
to forgive and be forgiven.

Still, we hunger now
for what you mercifully offer:
a new beginning in living fully,
loving generously, justicing passionately,
sharing peacefully, making merry inclusively.

Lord of atoms and galaxies,
societies, families, and these poor hearts of ours,
by your power and in your purposes,
begin this new creation in us today
and through every tomorrow,
liberating us to risk whatever
letting go and taking up it requires.

Unburden us from the guilt and self-pity,
the arrogance and defensiveness
that drains our energy to be compassionate
and our honesty to be humble.

Refresh our hope, renew our wonder,
expand our gratitude, sharpen our discernment,
nurture in us the will to be trustworthy
and the capacity to trust,
and make clear our vision
that we may see you in all we meet,
all we do, all we are, all we can become;
through Jesus Christ our Lord.
Amen.

We Hunger for What You Offer

Is This What It Means to Be Free?

Elusive yet attending God,
    here we are, as if you didn't know,
        bold to bother you again,
            since from the beginning
                you made us this way
                      and insisted on bothering us ever since.

Why do you bother us with all these questions,
    these counter claims, contingencies, and confusion,
        with the mystery in everything obvious
            and the hiddenness in everything plain?

Why all these whys, these ifs, hows, and whethers,
    all these half answers that multiply
        into more mind-wrinkling questions,
    all these nagging moral dilemmas
        instead of definite right and wrong solutions?

Why isn't the purpose of the universe evident, not obscured,
    by theories of relativity,
        principles of uncertainty
            and probability structures,
    by chaos dynamics,
        hints of a strange attractor,
    by antics of electrons in atoms
        and light that behaves like particles or waves,
            depending on who's watching?

PRAYERS OF REFLECTION

Why is the marvel of a molecule of DNA its capacity
   to blunder into something new
      when we would have made it perfect,
         according to our Eden complex,
            except the molecules blundered
               their way into us first—
or was that your "sort of" plan all the time,
   the blundering being a nudge
      toward an intentional choosing
         through the whole twisting way?

Why does the interaction of things and creatures
   constantly change things and creatures,
      which somehow makes us key players
         in your process of creating this corner
            of the universe, doesn't it?
        Or maybe of the whole thing?

Why is our compelling impulse to love
      so confusing and sometimes painful?
What makes our nagging need
   to do what's right and just
      so difficult and complicated?
Why is beauty so haunting and inviting,
   words so powerful and compelling,
feelings the bridge to neighbors and to stars?
      thought so deep and yet confounding,
music a universal language
      no one can quite explain or silence,
         unless the universe itself ceases to hum?

Is This What It Means to Be Free?

Why do you bother us in so many ways
    with so many mysteries?
Why suffering,
    why accidents and birth defects,
        why violence and hate,
            why disease and cruelty?
Why did you do it this way?

Why throw us out of Eden for one mistake?
    Or are we in exile because we *keep* making it?
Is this what it means to be free?
    Is freedom the foremost
        of your lover's gifts
to this whole megillah,
    from galaxies to microbes,
        to human hearts and minds and wills?

Quite honestly, it is a bothersome gift, Lord,
    a burden equal to its blessing
        in spite of our passionate desire for it,
    for from the Garden on, we seem hell bent
        on misunderstanding and misusing it,
            shirking its responsibilities,
                as well as its just possibilities,
        wanting more order and security,
            more privilege, comfort and control
                than freedom allows,
                    or love can give, or even faith can grasp,
        if the mysteries of this living universe
            reveal any of truth at all,
                or human history does.

Is This What It Means to Be Free?

So, Lord, we pray we're worth your bother
   and that you continue to be up to it,
      and we up to it as well,
   to what the gifts of love and freedom are about.
Bother us, then, into the wisdom
   of accepted limitations,
      of knowing that all we do not know
         is not a matter of "not yet,"
      but of what we will never know,
         are not meant to know,
            the not of not being you—
               putting all our pretense
                  at least momentarily aside.

Bother us out of pride
   into the humility of wisdom
      and into gentleness with each other
         and ourselves, and with you.

Bother us out of fear
   into the courage to take
      the leap of faith we've feared to take,
         falling not being our primal inclination,
            except, perhaps (where else at last)
               into your arms.

Lord, we know not why
   you bother us with freedom and with grace,
      with beauty and with awe,
   with children's trusting
      past our little answers,

Is This What It Means to Be Free?

      with their bothering us to follow them
          into the unknown, unknowable lands
              of their insistent curiosity
                  and on to kingdoms of dreams
              and ever after.

Bothered as we are, we do not pray
    to be delivered from any save the fear of it,
        but rather to be bothered on and on
            by our freedom, and by yours,
                into even deeper water,
                    so we will keep bothering you as well.

Our truest hope is that, in that interaction
      and the faith it requires,
    things will change,
        we will change,
           the world will change,
and there will be more cures,
      more symphonies and laughter,
          more peace and community,
more honesty and trust,
      more justice, more mercy,
          more reconciliation and rejoicing,
more reveling in the mystery
    of your unaccountable grace,
        more of gratitude,
           of life,
              of you.
            Amen.

Is This What It Means to Be Free?

We Yearn to Return to You

God of long-suffering love,
    since you have eternity
        you seem willing to wait while we wander,
            distracted by the pitch of a hundred hucksters.
    That's what your gift of freedom to us means.
So be less patient with us,
    for our awareness sharpens
        that our time is too short to waste any more.
We yearn to return to you,
    but need, want, ask you
        to break our infatuation with dabbling
            and with dodging the claims of your kingdom.
Disrupt our frittering ways
    harshly, painfully, if need be,
        lest our deep longing for life and love
            go forever unslaked.
Come now, Compelling Clarity,
    like the lode star into the fog of our chaos,
        that we may find ourselves
            and the way to you who dwells
                even in our sighs and tears,
                      our fretful stirring and weary running,
        that in our turning and returning,
            we be joined in the renewal of what you intended us to be,
                and find resilience in the mystery and simpleness of you,
            discovering, through the quietness and confidence,
                strength to walk and not faint
                    as we seek redirection and integration
                      of ourselves and with community
                  in the gracious silence and sureness of you.   Amen.

We Yearn to Return to You

Be New to Us Once More

From the vertigo
    of our whirligig banter and posturing,
        our slapstick of sufficiency,
            our crack-the-whip of confusion and fear,
  out of the deep-still center
    where our longing stirs,
        we lurch hopefully toward you.

Deliver us from the idolatry
    of our reflexive self-righteousness,
        our enshrined routines,
            our smug biases,
  for they have wearied
    and misled us,
  made you a stranger to us,
    a shadow at the margin
        of our frantically-driven days.

So we have become
    clever yet foolish,
        successful yet dissatisfied,
            likable yet lonely,
  hopeful yet resistant,
    charming yet vain,
        effusive yet profane,
            spiritual yet prayer-less.
  Weariness overwhelms us,
    renewal eludes us.

O God, please, do not weary of us.
   Draw near to us now,
      to forgive us,
         to loosen the strangle hold
            of our doubts,
        to trip up our strutting certainties,
           to unmagnify our fears
              heal our shame,
                comfort our impoverished spirits.

Set us free to forgive
   ourselves,
      each other,
         our enemies,
   and to forgive you
      for whatever grievances
         we bear against you,
   that we be reconciled.

Be new to us once more,
   that we become new for ourselves,
      and for each other
   and together try something new
      for you and in your world;
         for Jesus sake, and ours.
           Amen.

Be New to Us Once More

Meet Us in the Unexpected Places

Wily One,
    traces of your grace are strewn all through
        our schedule-puckered lives,
    and sometimes, on odd occasions,
        we stumble over them and realize,
            in a stunning, heartbeat moment,
        the mystery and majesty and claim
            of what we take for granted.

So we come to worship, to pray, to thank you.
    But more, we would not leave unchanged,
        comfortable in our familiar ways,
            our busily diminished days.

O God of our deepest discontent,
    grant us to recognize in the nag of our longing
        your Spirit working to break in and free us
            from the cages in which we too often put ourselves:
        the wearying rush, the politic word, lying congeniality,
            the strategies to succeed, the circular socializing,
        everything that contorts our humanity,
            closes our ears, glazes our eyes,
                wilts our hearts, pilfers our souls.

We know at our core, God of patient generosity,
    that our easier responses to your grace—
        the quick prayers, the brief span of worship,
            the shrug at sermons, the gifts of money—
                leave us impoverished still, and stuck.

Meet Us in the Unexpected Places

We ask to be stirred and disturbed
    toward something daring and sweaty and fun,
        outrageously, wonderfully soul-satisfying
    in the grace of your summons
        to love you and neighbor and enemy
            as we love our truest, free-est self.

Slow us, calm us, and ease us into being good samaritans
    to each other and to the poor, the abused, the forgotten,
        the outcast and rejected, the children and the aged,
            and those whose fear makes them obnoxious.

Make us bold to hold those in power accountable,
    to model generosity to the wealthy,
        humility to the arrogant,
            mercy to the self-righteous,
                compassion to the indifferent.

O wily God,
    meet us in the unexpected places
        of our daily round,
    and make us glad of heart
        in our tilt toward justice and joy
            in our families, our work, this church,
                this community, this nation,
    with this precious earth and human family
        you love so much that you press us
            to join you in pressing it
                a bit closer to your kingdom.
                    Amen.

Meet Us in the Unexpected Places

Pastoral PRAYERS

Keen Our Awareness

O God of all seasons and settings of our lives,
    sometimes our doubts and cynicism close down like a fog,
        and you seem far removed, leaving us vexed and lost.
    Then the music rises, the rain falls, rainbows slather on oily puddles,
        a baby giggles, someone stands for justice,
            the daily composes its poetry,
                and the fog lifts along with our spirits and our dreams.
    So we see again that it's all a gift from you,
        and our eyes glisten, our voices lift in praise to you.

O God of all creatures and contexts of your creation,
    sometimes we feel alone, isolated, cut off, of little consequence,
        and we find no trace at all of your presence.
    Then a friend calls, a letter arrives, a neighbor knocks, a child visits,
        and love becomes a word made flesh again, and we remember.
    So we sense once more that it's all a gift,
        and life becomes a *we* again, an *ours*, an *us*,
            and the *you* and *yours* of it is real again,
                the kingdom resonant in our midst. Thank you!

O God of healing and power,
    sometimes we feel exhausted, defeated, used up, ready to give up,
        and you seem altogether elsewhere and indifferent.
    Then a child looks at us through bottomless eyes,
        asks a forever question demanding an honest, for-now answer,
            and awe somehow tremors up our spines, levers our minds,
    and we know anew what this life is all about—
        you, and hope revived,
            and not giving in to temptation, being delivered from evil,
                and the kingdom, power and glory forever,
                    and love that, thank you, never ends.

Keen Our Awareness

O God of patience and of peace,
    more than sometimes we get damnably busy, and enchanted with it,
        over-reaching and insensitive, vain and irritable,
            careless of all else save paddling on the rapids
                of our self-preoccupation and ambition,
                    while being increasingly terrorized
                        by whirlpools of emptiness and regret,
                            feeling as if you have abandoned us
                                to our own fretful devices.

Then a chance to change
    bursts in the flash of a cardinal in the corner of our eye,
        floats in on the peach-pink lips of a pucker-up day like this,
            snuggles against us in bed, tickles us in a joke on ourselves,
                echoes in an adversary who criticizes us accurately,
                    confronts us in an exploited person's just challenge,
                      and the world swells with possibilities again,
    beauty brims over from its source,
        the universe asks to be noticed,
            grace teems round us like new galaxies,
the first wave comes singing in to our hearts,
    sets them to singing their own songs
        in the showers, in boardrooms,
            voting booths, and malls,
and compassion comes in on the second wave,
    courage on the third,
        commitment on the fourth,
            you and peace in them all.
                Thank you!

Keen Our Awareness

O God of ingenious purpose,
    sometimes our fears and doubts squeeze the air and aim from us
        until life seems pointless, drab and flat,
            dry-boned and disconnected,
        and even you seem unable or unwilling to hook it together again.
    Then some family members gather needy at day's end, and just talk;
        talk to each other, engage, disclose, ask,
            confront, fight, forgive, dare to love boldly,
    or a prayer flutters up in us like a feather off a ragtag angel,
        or in some gathering, like this worship,
            we get caught up, touched, singed,
    so when a neighbor, or an enemy, or one of the least of these
        shows up with a need, a claim, a bundle of grievances,
            the point we lose finds us again and our sleeves go up,
                and, thank you, the dry bones flex and connect.

O God of mercy and the marginalized,
    sometimes we get discouraged
        to the teetering edge of despair for the world
            shadowed by the pain of the sick and starving,
        the cries of the oppressed, the excluded and exploited,
            and the harsh judgments of those self-righteously ready
                to blame them for their plight,
    and we are frustrated
        that the need for our compassion
            exceeds our capacity,
    and that we are too weak to carry the burdens
        of these brothers and sisters
            you seem to have left to our care,
    and we complain
        that you ask more of us
            than we can manage.

Keen Our Awareness

Then a youngster hobbling down the street
   with braces and crutches,
      smiles at us as though he had no care in the world
         but the next step,
an ageless Down syndrome kid
   beams us up in the supermarket,
an anonymous old man with half his teeth missing
   asks how we are
      and tells us a story of his recent good fortune,
a homeless mother recovering from an addiction
   and fighting for her kids
      looks clear-eyed at us
         and talks trustingly of you and her future,
a teen-age prodigal
   stands up and starts for college and home,
a wedding gets dared,
   a hard birthing delivers a healthy baby,
some irrepressible samaritan shows up
   to sign us up as innkeepers,
and your irrepressible kingdom
   scatters a trace or two or a dozen or more
      for us to stumble over, pick up,
         let pick us up, and find an ease in, and a way.

So we learn again that what's up to us is not everything,
   but only the most we can do
      to make grace real to others and ourselves,
         to help justice roll down like waters,
            and peace flow like a river,
               and beauty spring out of ugliness,
                  and hope take wing like an eagle.

Keen Our Awareness

Now, O God,
   we pray on, labor on, love on, trust on
      with a confidence only a cross and an empty tomb
         can account for.
   Let the words we have raised in prayer,
      take root in our spirits
   and by the alchemy of grace
      turn to praise of you,
         to a swell of gratitude for your being there,
            for enduring our questions and complaints,
               for listening beyond them
                   to our marrow that misses you
                      when we wander,
                 to our hearts that long for you
                    through all we love,
                 to our minds that seek you
                    in every thought and question,
                      though mostly all unaware.

Be patient with us who surely try your patience,
   as you often try the short supply of ours,
      and as we always try our own.
   Keen our awareness so that we not go unscathed, indifferent,
      unaltered, or ungrateful through this world,
         or be unmoved by its wild, terrible, incredible beauty,
            and the aching need we can meet
               only as we meet each other.

Be merciful, Holy One, for without your mercy
   we could not live with ourselves or with each other,
      for we judge quickly and harshly,
         and the measure we give is the measure we get.

Keen Our Awareness

Touch and heal us, guide and challenge us,
> that in the calmness as in the turbulence,
>> we will sense your presence and seek your will.

In these, as in all our days of ferment and summons,
> we pray for our beloved country,
>> our leaders, citizens, critics, and those without advocates,
> that together we sift out the grain of what matters
>> from the chaff of power and privilege,
>>> act as those who discern
>>>> that you are at work with us
>>>>> in making the history of our time,
>>> and weigh wisely, calculate boldly, do justly,
>>>> and invest our little time and strength
>>>>> in those things that make straight your highway
>>>>>> by feeding the hungry,
>>>>>>> clothing the naked,
>>>>>>>> freeing the prisoner,
>>>>>>>>> and reflecting your kingdom coming.

O God, may we all grow in awareness
> of the ways you answer our prayers
>> through using us in answering the prayers
>>> of our brothers and sisters.
> So we will not miss your grace,
>> nor fail in creativity, nor falter in generosity
>>> as members of this ridiculous, sublime,
>>>> wounded, wonderful human family of yours,
>>>>> and of ours;
>>> by your grace, out of our gladness,
>>>> in Jesus' spirit we pray.
>>>>> Amen.

Keen Our Awareness

We Pray Because We Breathe

Eternal One,
    we often wander in our prayers,
        losing our way in a dozen distractions,
            jumbling thoughts, tripping over words.
    Yet we pray because we breathe,
        because we sing, and love and struggle.

We pray because we cannot still this longing for you,
    this urge to thank you, to ask your help,
        this holy nudge to seek you
            for what we cannot be or do without you.

We pray because we are yours,
    and beneath our bustle and clamor we know that.
        Lord, ease us now out of our shallowness
            into the deep waters of your grace.

We thank you for this mysterious gift of life,
    for all its songs and skirmishes
        its love-making, its haste-stopping beauty,
            its tender mercies, its honest dialogues,
    its stitching-together acts of compassion,
        its small celebrations and broad visions,
            its simple tastes of bread, its costly friendships,
    for the turn of words to unlock minds and move hearts,
        for kindnesses and chuckles,
            for the forthrightness of children
                who enlarge our sense of what is possible for us all.

O Compassionate Father-Mother,
   abide with us wherever we are, in whatever season,
     to enable our caring to be wise,
       our support honest, our concerns thoughtful,
        our loves as well as our fears be accurate,
       our spirits so open to your guidance
        that we will become faithfully daring,
         expectantly patient,
          responsibly hopeful
           with each other
            and with your people
              in our neighborhoods and nation.

Holy One,
   out of our weakness we turn to your terrible,
     wonderful, cleansing, gracious power.
   Deeper than our doubts we trust your promises,
     and so we pray for others we bear on our hearts.
   Comfort those who recently experienced the chill of sorrow.
     Fill the emptiness of those who feel forgotten or forsaken.
   Strengthen those who await the results of critical medical tests,
     and heal the bodies and spirits of those who are sick or injured.
   Abide with those whose days on earth dwindle down to a few,
     and grant them peace and the confidence that nothing
       can separate them from your love in Christ Jesus our Lord.
   Guide those who do business in this nation,
     that they be accountable not only for their profit
       but for all the peoples' welfare
     until we all join in efforts toward economic justice,
       stewardship of the environment,
         inclusion of the marginalized and oppressed.

We Pray Because We Breathe

Enlarge the partisan passion of our government's leaders
 into passion for justice for those caught in poverty and violence,
  and especially for the children of our land and of the earth,
 until we all learn that we are accountable for every child
  because each of them is truly your child,
   and we will be judged on how we care for them.

O Lord, you hold us in a love
 tough enough to embrace the cross
  and ingenious enough to empty the tomb.
 Deepen us in that love
  and make us ready for its sacrifices and surprises,
   ready partners with you
    in the work of redeeming your people
  and so in fulfilling your purposes for us
   and unfolding our hearts
    to the joy of your presence with us
   in all the days of our lives,
    and in all the prayers we lift to you,
     as we do this prayer
      and the one Jesus taught us to pray together,
       "Our Mother-Father who art in heaven . . ."

We Pray Because We Breathe

Prayers OF DEDICATION

Multiply Our Faith

O God of miracles and multiplications,
    in bringing these gifts
        we dare to measure ourselves
            not by our fears or failures or frailties,
                however large they seem,
            but by our hope and faith and love,
                however small they may be.

Now we pray that by your grace
    we, our boldness, and our gifts
        will become miracles of leaven
            in the lump of this world.

Multiply our courage
    that we may be a source of life
        and justice and peace
             for those we carry in our hearts,
                and on our consciences.

Multiply our faith in you
    that all our struggles, all our joys
        will be steps taken toward what it means
        to be human,
            to be sisters and brothers,
                and to be yours;
                    through Christ our Lord.
                    Amen.

Multiply Our Faith

Teach Us Again and Again

O God, be with those
    for whom these gifts are given,
  and bless us who give them
    that we may dedicate ourselves as well,
      and passionately move against the ugliness
        and injustice and violence in your world
          without becoming unjust or ugly or abusive.

Teach us again and again
  that the reward for loving
    is having our capacity to love stretched
      to include even those we define as enemies.

So would we dare to live as vagabonds of faith,
  risking something big for something right,
    challenging all that shrinks and separates people,
      pressing on toward the freedom
        that enlarges life by sharing it
          with all our brothers and sisters,
            and empowers us not to be afraid;
              in Christ's name and spirit.
                Amen.

Teach Us Again and Again

Keep Us in Your Fierce Love

Spendthrift God,
    past all explanation or deserving,
        we have received from you
            grace upon grace upon grace.
Though many come disguised,
    each one blesses, challenges, bewilders,
        supports, stretchs, comforts us,
though none protect us
    from the struggles of life
        and that, too, is cause for thanksgiving,
for neither do they quarantine us from
    courage, compassion, creativity,
        and our consciousness of
            deep communion of our common life.

So we ask you to bless us and all our gifts,
    keeping us in your fierce love
        as we strive for your kingdom
            and receive from you the things we need;
    increasing by your merciful love
        the good for which you intend our gifts,
            and which we yearn for them to do;
    and nurturing by your sneaky love
        those brothers and sisters, neighbors and enemies,
            we live with in this human family
                and for whom we give so much less generously
                    of the grace and joy we have received,

until, through your stubborn love,
    we open our hearts and minds
        to the ancient tidings of peace on earth,
    to the summons for justice to roll down like waters,
        and righteous like an ever-flowing stream,
    and we respond to that tidings and summons daily
        making them a bit more real
            on this precious, whirling globe,
    adding our joy to yours
        as a small gift from us
    in return for your great gift to us
        of amazing grace that has brought us safe thus far,
            and day by day will lead us home.
                Amen.

Keep Us in Your Fierce Love

Prayers
FOR A FEW SPECIAL OCCASIONS

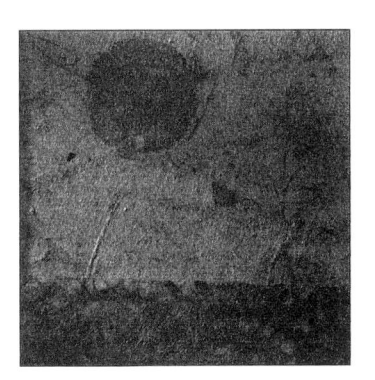

ADVENT

We Watch and Wait for You

Hidden God,
    wherever you are
        in your own kind of space,
            we watch and wait for you
                to startle us to wakeful newness
                    in this Advent season.

Come and thrust into us
    the spirit of daring and courage
        to make flesh on earth
            a bit of the kingdom of heaven.

Come to open the inns
    of our minds and hearts
        to the miracles of your compassion
            and purpose as Jesus demonstrated them.

Come and make your own transforming way
    in the desert of our confusion
        and wilderness of me and mine,
            so we may walk with Jesus the hard way
                of justice, mercy, and peace among the people of earth.

Come and lift up the valleys
   of our discouragement and doubt and denial,
      and make level the mountains of our greed and pride,
         so we may see your glory revealed once more
            in us and in all our brothers and sisters,
               from the shepherd least to the magi lofty.

Come and fulfill through us Mary's vision
   of mercy stretching to all generations,
      of the proud scattered, the powerful punctured,
         of the rich emptied and the poor filled,
            and our lives magnifying your grace.

Come lace our songs, our shopping, our celebrations
   with your mystery and strange magnificence,
      and let us sense it in the small, strange stirrings
         of the earth and of our hearts, now and always.
         Amen.

We Watch and Wait for You

ADVENT

Gentle Us Open

Lord of Life and Light,
    help us not to fall in love
        with the darkness that separates us
            from you and from each other,
    but to watch large-eyed, wide-hearted,
        open-handed, eager-minded for you,
            to dream and hunger and squint and pray
                for the light of you and life for each other.

Lord, amidst our white-knuckled,
    furrow-faced busy-ness in this season,
        we realize deep within us that your gifts
            of mercy and light, peace and joy, grace upon grace
                can be received only if we are unclenched open.

So this is our prayer, Lord: Open us!
    Gentle us open, pry, shock, tickle, beguile, knock,
        amaze, squeeze, any wily way you can us open.

Open us to see your glory
    in the coming again of the light of each day,
        the light in babies' eyes and lovers' smiles,
            the light in the glaze of weariness that causes us to pause,
                the light of truth wherever spoken and done.

Open us to songs of angels in the thumping of traffic,
    in the rustle of shoppers, the canopy of pre-dawn silence,
        in the hum of hope, the wail of longing within us,
            in the cries of our brothers and sisters for justice and peace,
                and in our own souls' throb toward goodness.

Gentle Us Open

Open us, then, to share the gifts you have given us
   and to the deep yearning to share them gladly and boldly,
      to sweat for justice, to pay the cost of attention,
         to initiate the exchange of forgiveness,
            to risk a new beginning free of past grievances,
               to engage with each other in the potluck of joy
   and to find the gifts of a larger love and deeper peace.

Open us, Lord of miracles of the ordinary,
   to the breath-giving, heart-pounding wonder of birth,
      a mother's fierce love, a father's tender fidelities,
         a baby's barricade-dissolving burble and squeak,
that we may be born anew ourselves
   into the "don't be afraid" fullness of your image,
      the fullness of a just and joyful human community,
         the fullness of your kingdom,
            in the fullness of your time;
         through the eternal grace of
               your son, our brother Jesus.
            Amen.

Gentle Us Open

MARTIN LUTHER KING, JR., SUNDAY

Keep Us Faithful to Your Dream

O God of all nations and peoples,
   we are grateful for the dreams
      of freedom, justice, and peace
         forever spun by your Spirit
            and focused by prophets in every age.

We are grateful that in our time
   you call every man and woman
      to lift up and live by that dream,
         to embody it in our world by
      walking the walk,
         confessing our complicities
            braving the work,
               daring the confrontation,
   exposing the lies,
      singing our faith,
         asking the questions,
   raising the Cain,
      making the sacrifices,
         organizing the community,
   easing the hate,
      expanding the compassion.
         enduring in humility,
   risking the revolution of love,
      and ratifying the 'not for sale' sign on our souls.

We especially praise you this day
   for the life of Martin Luther King, Jr.,
      and for countless others down the ages
         whose names are known and unknown,
      and for those who yet lift up the dream and confirm it as yours,
         who quicken the conscience of this country
            and the human family around this globe,
      whose courage and commitments,
         vision and enthusiasm and joy
            brace our spirits and fire our wills.

So we thank you and remember
   and move boldly on in the faith that,
      however dark the night,
         however fearful the tyrannies of oppression,
            however heavy the weight of arrogance,
   we can yet be confident and buoyant in you and your promise
      that one day justice will roll down like waters
         and righteousness like an ever-flowing stream
            and peace abide in our hearts,
               through this land,
                  on this earth
      between brothers and sisters of every race,
         every nation, every faith, every orientation,
            every generation, every wounded, wonderful
               one and all of your human family.

Keep us faithful to that promise,
   your dream,
      and for Christ's sake, and for ours.
         Amen.

Keep Us Faithful to Your Dream

A MUSIC SERVICE

Tune Us Again to the Timeless, Timely Words

O God of awesome beauty,
    you taught the stars to sing
        yet the heavens cannot contain your glory
            nor this place your holiness,
    nor our words and music
        carry to you our gladness in your presence,
            our wonder at your tender mercies,
                our gratitude for your grace.

We rejoice that you join with us now
    as we gather in your name
        to sing your praise
            in this rousing season of resurrection.
Deepen and enthrall us with the music
    you have composed in our spirits,
        sounded in our hearts,
            set on our lips,
                played through our fingers
                      to echo your image in us.

Tune us again to the timeless, timely words
    and visions and spirit of the psalmists
        that we may be delighted and redirected
            through the gifts of music and musicians,
        rejoice at the mysterious link of songs and souls,
            be eased in our fretful stir and anxious thoughts,
                renewed in our trust and love of you,
                    and inspired in our service of your human family.

Tune Us Again to the Timeless, Timely Words

Lift us by your creating and compassionate Spirit
    that we may catch the strains of your kingdom's chorus,
        be recruited to join it, however off-key our efforts,
    and composed to expand our worship and witness
        from this enchanting place and time
            to the risky, creative, celebrative embrace
                of all our sisters and brothers on this earth
                    you are always and forever making new
                        in the ongoing resurrection of Jesus, and us.
                    Amen.

Tune Us Again to the Timeless, Timely Words

A WEDDING

Thank You for This Weaving of Lives

Gracious God, thank you for this day
    and for the mysterious and serendipitous way
        you have woven together the lives of ____ and ____;
    for all that made this day dawn first in promise and hope,
        now in deep love and commitment.
Thank you for the families of _____ and ____,
    for out of their love and nurture this moment has come.
Thank you for these friends here gathered to celebrate and bless
    the sacred joy of this moment.

Thank you for all _____ and ____ have shared, and will share,
    of laughter and tears, thoughts and dreams,
        slammed doors and open arms,
            noisy parties and quiet walks,
                whispers, songs, and screams,
                      hard decisions and gentle caresses,
        and for your presence that makes such sharing holy.

O God, be with them in all their tomorrows
    as you have been with them in all their yesterdays,
        and help them not to be afraid.

Grant them such vision as will enable them to take risks,
    to forsake security for integrity,
        to fear not to fail at all else save love.

Give them such dreams as will enable them
    not to make peace with what does not give peace,
        and to willingly sacrifice comfort for growth, ease for intimacy.

Thank You for This Weaving of Lives

Help them to learn the hard lessons of love,
> that, more than how we feel,
>> love has to do with how we act toward one another.

Grant them to learn that justice is love with its sleeves rolled up,
> to learn to pick up daily the pieces
>> of what taking for granted breaks
>>> and what self-preoccupation shatters
>>>> and put them together again,
> to do the soul-callousing, gutsy work required
>> to treat the other person fairly,
>>> to credit them sensitively,
>>>> to speak to them honestly,
>> to build trust in the realization that without trust
>>> love withers and intimacy flees away.

So, enable them to say what they mean
> and mean what they say to each other,
>> even though it mean disagreements and arguments,
> for hot arguments lead to more intimacy
>> than cold resentments and sullen silences.

Be with them as they learn that trust does not require agreement
> but rather deep exchange,
>> genuine mutuality,
>>> lived equality.

Gracious God, grant to ____ and ____ laughter and perspective
> in the awareness that life is never quite as serious as we suppose,
>> but grant as well, that their laughter be grounded
>>> in love more precious than they dare to take for granted,
>>>> even for a day.

Thank You for This Weaving of Lives

Most especially grant them
> to root their love in trust of your love,
>> and to know that theirs are not the only resources
>>> at work in their relationship.

Grant them the grace to forgive each other's failures and faults,
> and the wisdom to know how and when
>> to release each other into your keeping.

Finally, Lord, grant them passion that they may never be too careful,
> that they may have the wisdom of children,
>> who know that to believe is to see kingdoms,
> and the wisdom of fools,
>> who find miracles in surprising places and persons and times.

Grant them passion for each other,
> for life, for truth and peace and justice and beauty,
>> for finding those treasures of joy you have buried
>>> in the fields they will plow daily, and so
> passion for moving on, confident in themselves,
>> in each other, and in you,
> passion in knowing that to say, " 'I love you'
>> means 'Let the revolution begin' "; *
>>> through Jesus Christ our Lord.
>>>> Amen.

*Quote from a sermon by Carter Heyward.

Thank You for This Weaving of Lives

CONFIRMATION

They Are Gifts to Us

We are delighted, God,
    by the fabulous hocus-pocus of Spring
        tip-toeing up around us on soft petals
            of lavender and pink, green and gold.

Yet even this creep of splendor
    does not measure so well your grace
        as the stunning hocus-pocus of children
            who grow up among us
and become incredible young men and women,
    such as these special ones
        who this day join hearts with us as your disciples.
They are gifts to us, each one of them,
    as all our children are,
        gifts of promise, of hope, of mystery, of love,
            gifts of the richness, excitement, and challenge of life itself.

Generous God,
    the extravagance of all your gifts eludes our words,
        and too often even our awareness,
    yet we are freshly reminded of them
        by these beloved of our hearts,
            these offspring of our bodies and our dreams.
We thank you for their lives, and for our own lives,
    a bit more worn but no less splendiferous.
We thank you for the sure, subtle ways of your grace,
    for it is you who weaves into them, and us,
        such immeasurable worth and incredible possibility.

They Are Gifts to Us

It is you, Awesome One,
   who makes our lives such a glad dare,
      such a whirl of struggle and ease,
         creativity and carelessness,
            triumph and defeat,
               joy and pain,
                  knowledge and wisdom,
                     striving and wandering,
                        mercy and mystery,
all of it opening out and leading to you,
   all of it calling us
      to all the commitment and honesty,
         all the gladness and gratitude,
         all the prayer and fidelity,
            all the outrageousness and integrity,
               all the humility and risk we can muster,
all of it strangely assuring us
   that we can trust that you are at work
      in and through and around us
         beyond our capacity
            to fully understand or imagine.

We thank you and ask for one grace more:
   that together with these you entrust to us,
      we keep learning to trust your assurance
      and to be less afraid.

O God, even as you spin stars into galaxies,
   so do you spin us into families.
We pray now for our particular families,
   especially those of these young persons,
      and for the family of the church,
      and for the human family.

They Are Gifts to Us

So Father-Mother of us all,
>   give us wisdom and patience
>   to share our lives deeply
>   that we may be a blessing to each other
>   and to the human family.

In Christ Jesus you have given us and our children
>   a vision of what it is to be human and faithful,
>   to be true and just, bold and beautiful.
>   Grant to them and to us
>   the nerve to hold and embody that vision
>   so that together we make our way,
>   and the kingdom's way, in the world.

And since you know, O God, that way is often hard,
>   grant us courage that we falter not
>   in our commitment to what sustains
>   and enlarges life for all people.
>   In your own way, make these young people, and us,
>   so deeply aware of your presence with us
>   that we may be free to travel light,
>   to take time for quietness,
>   to find healing in laughter at ourselves,
>   and to take nothing for granted,
>   especially not the love that links us to each other,
>   to you, and to your purposes for us,
>   which are deeper and steadier
>   even than the roll of seasons
>   and the glitter of the stars.

They Are Gifts to Us

Wild and wonderful God,
   may we rejoice to strive for your kingdom first,
      to care faithfully and tenderly for the earth,
         to stand against anything that trivializes or
            dehumanizes any human being for any reason,
               especially the children of the earth.

Shake us, wake us, and empower us,
   and the leaders of church and nation,
      to rejoice in all our children,
         and to dare to be for them,
            and do with them,
      everything possible to give them
         the chance to live fully, freely,
            openly and inclusively,
               creatively and generously,
      lest by indifference or callousness,
         or the insidious chomp and gnaw of busy-ness,
            we lose our own chance to live fully and freely.

In the spirit of Jesus who keeps growing among us,
   that we may keep growing
      into the hocus-pocus fullness of your grace
         and glory, and in whose name we pray.
            Amen.

They Are Gifts to Us

Narrative PRAYERS

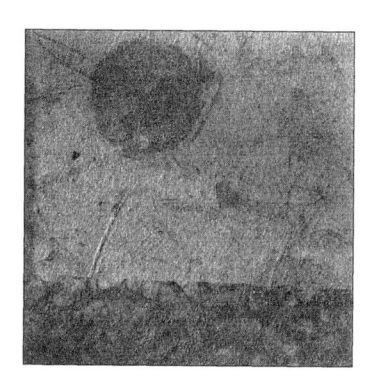

The Only Answer-Choice There Is

O God of the great sweep of history,
    and yet of the wee tracings
        of the histories of each one of us,
I would go over again with you
    this recent bit of mine
        to fix it in my heart and mind,
    to track once more the markers of grace
        and where they took me,
    and might take me still, dare I follow them.

It happened early evening last, you already know,
    when the curtain of a long day
        was slowly being drawn,
    and I was driving back from shared tears,
        sharp expletives, a stammered prayer,
    feeling more than half angry at the ugly pathology report
        conveyed so matter-of-factly to my too-young friend
by a white-smocked, stethoscope-swaddled messenger,
    the news scorching like senselessness,
churning up a whirlwind of feardust dark as death,
    the threat of those matter-of-damn-fact words,
like a cosmic question mark hurling from no-seeming-where,
    like a meteor hitting earth's heart and blotting out the sun,
seeming thus to smother the whole enterprise of life,
    twisting beauty terribly awry.

Waiting for the demonically slow stoplight,
    I whispered to myself and whoever else might be listening
        to the jumble of me, which by more than chance you were,
    "What is it about, this so-called
        'matter-of-factness' of life and death?"

I don't know what made me right then
   turn my dazed gaze upward
      for the first time in too long a while,
where, from beyond the stoplight,
   part of an answer spied me:
a matter-of-fact shining silver sliver
   of a new moon winked there
        (or was it a feather from an angel's wing?)
   floating in a sky full of air,
      clear as a child's prayer, or laugh,
        which perhaps is the same thing.

I managed a small smile
   at that sliver of coincidence
      until another one occurred,
        my also out-of-nowhere memory
          of something a friend said once:
"A coincidence is what happens
   when God wants to remain anonymous."
      I ask you, "Could that be true?"

Anyway, remember, by then evening had shaded
   into pale sapphire, light enough but barely to uncover
      the all-day-long missed dogwood leaf
        cradled in my windshield wiper,
   a tiny yet immeasurable mystery of maroon,
      the color of holiness resting there like a sacrament,
        like a piece of sunrise that had broken off
          to carry a "this is my blood" word
            to wherever it happened to land,
this time in sight of me, like mercy,
   like the first drop of rain to break a drought.
      Could it be a non-coincidence for those with eyes to see?

The Only Answer-Choice There Is

Then, I can see it now, and of course you can, too,
   a beat before the light turned green,
      a mother just off the belching bus scurried to cross,
pulling a toddler behind her, pushing a stroller ahead,
      daring anyone to challenge her right of way,
which no one did, a minor miracle in a no-holds-barred city.
      Lord, how did that happen?
In the stroller was an infant crying
      for any of the dozen reasons you could name.
The mother limped, whether from a blister
      or weariness or infirmity, it didn't matter,
for whichever was no match for the fierceness of her.
      Yet not even her will or blustery commands
could quiet the wailing child or speed the towed one.

But here's the wonder, as you no doubt know.
   A dog trotted from out of somewhere—
      a nearby yard? a garbage can?
No matter, it joined the cross-the-street parade,
      trotting gimp-legged, too, alongside the stroller.
The exasperated mother stopped mid-crossing,
      never mind the traffic, and began to shout
to shoo the sniffing dog away.
   The dog just wagged and looked at her,
more in sympathy than in fright, I'd say,
      and turned to lick the crying baby's face
as if it were his own beloved pup.
      The crying stopped as if a switch had been flipped.
Then the giggle began, became a duet, then a trio,
      among the babe, the tickled mother, and the towed one behind.
So the waters of panic were parted by a canine Moses,
      and shortly the exodus continued while we,
         the Pharaoh's legions, watched.

The Only Answer-Choice There Is

I laughed as well, and surely you heard it,
    for on the snappy autumn air it carried clear
        as the aforementioned child's prayer,
            which my laugh, half-intended, was.
    And I wondered, slightly mystified, if grace
        doesn't slather us somewhat like a lapping dog?

So now, with you, I wonder the more, recalling that in the Bible,
        the Book of Hebrews says, with curious latitude,
    "Do not neglect to show hospitality to strangers,
        for by doing that, some have entertained angels
            without knowing it."
    And there it is again, in Holy Writ, that all too familiar
        "without knowing it," which surely covers
            more than half of all we hit or miss of it.
So now I ask you, Lord, not altogether facetiously,
    "Could it be that angels might have wagging tails?"
I suppose it doesn't pay to calculate the odds of that too closely,
    or to calculate the odds of any other miracles too closely either.

"How perilous is it to choose
    not to love the life we're shown?"
    So Irish Bard Seamus Heaney asks,
        and I cannot get shuck of that question, Lord,
because it's as if it is your own.
    Perilous in the extreme, I suppose my answer'd be.

As I drove on home, I thought of my young friend
    and the pathology report of serious metastasis,
and then the wink of the new moon and the dogwood leaf,
    the limping hassled mother and the stranger angel dog.
I realized, thank you, Lord, that life is the whole of it,
    and it's perilous indeed to choose
        not to embrace the life we're shown.

The Only Answer-Choice There Is

Yet choosing is so blessed hard to do without each other.
   My friend's eyes blazed when I left her in her antiseptic room.
      "I know God's in this," she said, "as you've said many times.
   And I know love never ends. Thanks for yours and God's."
      "You're welcome for mine, even more for God's," I said.
   I said it without thinking, and I'm not sure why I did,
      except now I wonder if the words weren't really mine.
   Who am I to speak for God, save this once?

But I know this, God, as well do you the more:
   What breaks the heart is love.
      Without it who would give a damn?
   I believe, God, what defines us is the mystery of that,
      and the struggle and the simplicity of it,
         like a mongrel dog, or the mongrel heart, of each of us.
   That we comprehend grace at all
      is nearly as incomprehensible
         as bread and flour and yeast raising into bread,
      as pain turning to wisdom, as struggle transposed to strength,
         as death transformed into a joke on the devil.
   And yet, by grace, I have seen those things happen,
      not, I trust, entirely a coincidence.

Looking back, and a step or two ahead,
   I see, Lord, in the light of you, that love is the struggle
      and there is no abandoning it.
   The struggle of it tutors the soul
      and transforms notes to music,
   bad news into irrepressible confidence,
      like that of a chemo-bald child
   singing nursery rhymes to herself at midnight
      in the pediatric intensive care unit as I listened.
   No coincidence, but gifts I took notice to accept.

The Only Answer-Choice There Is

I will stay with my friend and pray,
   and perhaps learn with her to not be afraid.
I do believe life is full of angels to entertain
   but not altogether unaware.
To embrace them and whatever they bring
     surely is part of what it means to avoid the peril
        of not choosing the life we're shown,
           or not choosing you who shows it to us.

That's not quite all, you know;
   it goes on to end and begin with
      this morning, while I was sitting on a bench
         in front of the bakery, sipping coffee
in air nip stubbornly defiant of the early sun,
   an old black man, limping, gnarled,
      stepped out gingerly from the store.
"O Lord," he sighed to no one in particular.
   "Amen," I responded particularly.
      He looked at me and nodded.
He struggled by as if he had all his years in tow
   and only that one day ahead.
Once by, between gimpy steps he turned and said,
   "The Lord is good, isn't he?"

"Yes," is the only answer I could give.
   I give it again now, Lord, in tearful gratitude,
      with this lump-in-the-throat prayer
         but smiling, too, waiting perhaps
            for the confirmation of a dog.
   O God, you've made the mystery
      of this life we're shown very wondrous deep,
         but "Yes" is really, first and last,
            the only answer-choice there is.   Amen.

The Only Answer-Choice There Is

This Wrestle Through the Night

Lord, the night may be bright as day for you,
    but it's definitely not for me.
        So here I am at 3 A.M.
    trying to learn again in the darkness
        the dangers and lessons
            of exaggerated expectations
                and humiliating disappointments.
Where were you, my Cosmic Friend,
    when I went to read and sign my new book
        in the big-time bookstore at the hot-shot mall?

You don't have to tell me, I know too well:
        It's a stupid question, hardly worth the asking.
    But it's the one that cried out of my heart
        when I'd expected at least a decent,
somewhat eager crowd
    and only three showed up
        (and two were family).
Please, don't laugh! I may myself someday,
    but not yet. The shame of it's too fresh.
        Just hear me out, so I can find my way
            through this mocking maze
                in which I'm groping.

Okay, it's no big thing to get knocked down
    a few pegs, I know that, and supposedly
        it could be good for me.
    And who doesn't know (certainly not you or even me)
        that this is a trifling matter,
            even on a scale of very minor things.

This Wrestle Through the Night

But, to be honest—
   and what's the point of not being?—
      I still feel discouraged and demeaned,
         simmering in self-pity, which I know is . . .
   all right, I'll say it so you won't need to,
      unworthy is the fair and fitting word, I guess.
Hey, I swear, it's the truth of me right now,
   and there's just you and me here anyhow,
      and even though you know it anyway,
         I have to pour it out,
            see it for myself,
               and that's the point, after all.

So, Lord, here's the question
   I keep coming back to: What is enough?
      The naked truth is I didn't get much
         of what I wanted, just a tiny fraction.
Maybe life works like that for most of us,
   just the fruit of one more tree
      is what we want,
         even if it's beyond our reach,
            or should be, given our limitations
               of the knowledge of good and evil,
                  plus the worm of greedy ambition
                     chomping near our core.
Yet, *ought* is seldom *is*,
   I don't have to tell you that,
      and there's the seed of disappointment,
         isn't it? I didn't get much
            of what I wanted.
So what's enough?

This Wrestle Through the Night

I'm thinking, Lord,
    thoughts that flood in now on the tide of weariness,
        the debris of the day and of myself,
            the driftwood of thoughts and images
                that come from I know not where
                    but only that they ride this wave of night.

I am thinking now of
    the countless times I've watched the sun rise
        like your mercy to gently lift the dark blanket
            from the earth and from my spirit,
    and the countless more times I've watched the sun set
        in such a splendiferous farewell
            it must reflect the fringe of your robe.
I've seen the sky define blue and endless.
    I've felt rain splatter on my face, white-water furious,
        yet sometimes gentle as a lisping child's spray,
    and I've experienced snow falling like peace on the earth
        and white to cover scarlet sins.

God, bewitching Friend you are,
    for I'm bewitched to thinking and remembering
        here all that, and this:
I've watched rivers run to the sea,
    full as life runs to you.
I've felt the wind blow like your Spirit
    to ripple grass on the prairies and hills,
and watched storms split the heavens
    with jagged arcs of power.
I've felt the sea roll in with the caress of assurance,
    of no-nonsense power and the eternal note of mystery,
        as roll in these thoughts and memories.

This Wrestle Through the Night

I've scratched the ears of dogs,
    laughed at the ballet of cats and monkeys,
        elephants and pelicans and dolphins.
I've heard the cry and gurgle of the newborn,
    played with children, rocked with grandmothers,
        learned from hundreds of teachers,
            some of them homeless, poor, and uneducated.
I've been awakened to beauty and life by Bach, Bernstein,
    Streisand, and mockingbirds and a score more.
I've seen the world re-created by Michelangelo, O'Keeffe,
    Pollock, my friend Ed Kerns, third-grade finger painters,
        and several dozen others.
I've been enlarged ten times squared by writers
    from Shakespeare to Toni Morrison
        and yet countless other storytellers,
            some in delis and diners, taverns and buses,
                churches and curb sides and prison cells.

I have tasted bread and wine,
    hot dogs and caviar,
        somehow in the alchemy
            of need and gift and joy
                all made holy
                    as your own overflowing banquet,
        even as these thoughts, visions, memories
            overflow now to nurture me
                from some mysterious place
                    beyond my pitiful self's capacity.
I've danced at parties,
    held hands with the dying.
I've loved and been loved and forgiven
    beyond all deserving, and all breath to tell of it,
        by family and friends and you.

This Wrestle Through the Night

I've been inspired and challenged by Martin Luther King, Jr.,
    Rosa Parks, Martin Buber, Nelson Mandela, Mother Teresa,
        Niebuhr, Rabin, Sadat, Heisenberg, Hawking,
      and every friend and enemy I've ever had.
I've been on dozens of Civil Rights Marches
    and trips to Central America and Haiti and South Africa
      in the cause of human rights, and every time
        it is I who have been set a bit more free.

I've been shaken, changed, blessed a thousand times, and still,
    by the prophets, and by Christ, and I've felt your touch, God,
      each time before I knew that's what it was.
I've been shrunk and stretched at the same time
    by the scatter of stars and found North in one of them.
I've experienced the loneliness of freedom and being human
    and having hard choices.
I've known the thrill of small triumphs,
    the instruction of painful defeats,
      and so the amazement of being part
        of the incredible human pilgrimage
          from Adam and Eve to the twenty-first century.
I've shared in the cantankerous yet remarkable family of faith.
    I'm conscious of being conscious and alive.

And, God, I see now all that's just for starters.
    How much is enough to be thankful
      and humbled to some saving symmetry?
    I see I have a couple of trips around the Milky Way
      past enough for that, no matter
        if I never receive another thing.

This Wrestle Through the Night

So I say it for you once again,
    for surely it's your word to me:
        Get on with it, my little friend,
            and thank me that you can.

I do thank you, my tough, strange Friend,
    for this wrestle through the night
        and the blessing you have crimped
            into my mind and soul.

Now I rasp a fond 'be well' to you,
    and pray with all my chastened heart
        that this lesson lasts, its glimmers coalesce
            enough for me to live more fully in your light.
                Amen.

This Wrestle Through the Night

Personal
PRAYERS

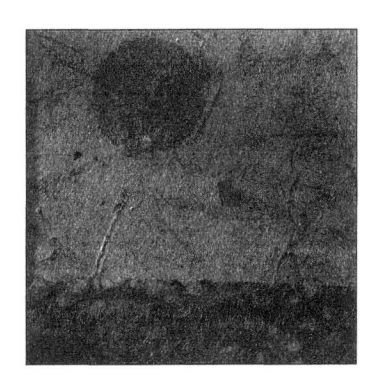

Help Me to Trust that Joy Is a Hint

God, often you hide in too much mystery.
   So before I pray my gratitude,
     please help me with this squelching quandary!

There are times when earth's morning's breath
   is honeysuckle, cedar, new snow, early bakery,
     and the air is soft as baby skin, silky as inner thigh;
  when the light glistens around like lover's eyes,
    or the moon's glowing sliver face is shadowed
      by the caress of the tender hand of this blue-orb lover;
  when a little girl waves from her window,
    oblivious school-bound teens entwine hands,
      leaving a ramble of profound silliness in their wake;
        in reply an old man sweeps his sidewalk in waltz rhythm,
          sparrows chirp their bacchanalian refrain;
  when time stretches out catlike as a delicious promise,
    my best friend slip-slides playfully to my side,
      throws an arm over my shoulder,
        and giggles as with the too-much-wine of it.

Then the joy fills me like an unspeakable glory,
   grace becomes sensual, and I am teary grateful,
     for a sweet, tender, precious moment . . .
until some waspish worry buzzes its threat of loss,
   the fiendish reminder of the inevitable passing of this gift,
     like the quick sad awareness of mortality after making love;
  or until the smirking piper of my puritanical legacy
    toots out the price that supposedly must be paid
      for such an amazing blessing as this beauty,
     this undeserved outpouring of the unutterably sacred,
      this motherly assurance of okay-ness,

    too soon turning to a wrestle with the slippery demons of dread,
        the chalk on blackboard of soul-storms
            that screeches the teeth and spine
                to the shivering edge of funk;
or until comes the sticky tar of guilt
    to pitch my spirit, staining the innocence of the loveliness,
        damning me for the indulgence of enjoying anything much
            when so many others are painfully sick or hungry
                or oppressed, deprived, beaten down
                    by poverty or drugs or deforming birth defects,
                      or bear the wounds
                          I myself have inflicted on them.

Why is joy so perishable, Lord?
    Help me with this,
        with all that takes the edge off joy,
            that pounces on it, like a drooling hunter,
                to bring it down, maul it to senseless bits,
            ridicules as a joke belief in beauty that does not fade
                or scoffs at reveling in an experience of anything
                    that will not last in this survival-of-the-fittest world,
            and so trusts only heartless, constant competition
                and prizes the wary awareness
                    that never for a moment
                        will the wolf lie down with the lamb.

Why, Lord, must joy be tainted with guilt, with fear,
    with intimations of death,
        with the swallow-it-up of sin, or evil,
            or the dog-eat-dog of things?
        Help me with this.

Help Me to Trust that Joy Is a Hint

Deliver me from feeling wrong when I am glad,
> or disturbed by bliss or saddened by beauty,
>> Help me with this, please!

Help me to trust, Lord,
> that the longing unleashed by joy will be fulfilled,
>> that it is not a joke, a cruel illusion,
> or else henceforth immunize me to it
>> lest it only break my heart.

But wait, Lord! Do not immunize me.
> Joy cannot be a joke, nor pain the end of it.
>> I think of Jesus, of the cross, of all the crosses
>>> on the landscape of history,
>>>> what mysterious resurrections came from them,
>>>> and surely, sneakily, come still.
>> Is it true, it must be true,
>>> you've made it so, haven't you,
>>>> as what we see through a glass darkly now,
>>> that pain and scuffle, loss, anguish, and tears,
>>>> suffering endured, shared, contested, prayed through,
>>>>> become the door that opens out to joy.

And yet, by the light of you, I begin to see that's but half of it.
> Joy is a swinging door
>> that opens back into the pain and scuffle,
>>> the sharing of suffering that makes us human
>>>> as Jesus was human, as you will us to be,
>>> for compassion is the hinge on which the door swings,
>>>> so we take the might and hope of joy back into the fray
>>>>> with sacrifice and gratitude the way,
>>>>>> joy pivoting toward bits and pieces become a feast,
>>>>>> enough to feed us all.

Help Me to Trust that Joy Is a Hint

God, help me with this quandary turning on itself.
  Help me to trust that joy is a now hint
    of what throbs imperishably
      at the heart of eternity,
        in your heart, your purposes,
  and that all things set against it, gnawing at it,
    all the pain, suffering, corruption, exploitation,
      all blood-letting and violence, cruelty and disease
        are what is perishable and will pass away,
or, truer, will be folded into your heart,
  transformed, changed, redeemed, as will I,
    and that is the deepest joy in the flickery glory
      of moments like this
        and those you sprinkle on us
          in such excessive, endless ways,
      gifts to be accepted,
        walked with,
          walked through
            in the gladness and gratitude of these
              humble, wondering, timidly brave,
                falteringly faithful hearts of ours.
              Amen.

Help Me to Trust that Joy Is a Hint

I Have Only So Much Time

I'm impatient, Lord,
    and it drives me crazy,
        to say nothing of those around me.
But you don't seem to have deadlines, God.
    Who would set them, after all?
        You have eternity.
           I don't!
So, forgive me, I want quick miracles,
    quick miracles of healing,
        of reconciling, of changing for good,
           of justice rolling down *now*,
    and of peace coming to the world, to my heart,
        of water turning into wine,
           grief and rage turning into joy
               within at most a season's breath.

Quick miracles, Lord, not slow ones,
    which are your specialty, it seems,
        so slow people die in the meantime,
           and children starve, are shot,
    storms and droughts destroy,
        hate and indifference flourish,
           cruelty rules the day,
    my life slips away.
        Life is short!
           I have deadlines!

I am not a patient person.
    I have only so much time to strive,
        to accomplish what I have to do,
           to right some wrongs, to make amends,

    to create some beauty, help the poor,
        welcome the outcast gays,
            clear the ghettos, repair the city,
only so much time—I'm not God, you know.
Maybe that's the dis-ease
    for which impatience is the symptom,
        I'm not God and I forget it,
            act compulsively as though I know
                what needs doing and when,
                    as though I am you,
                        a faithless confusion, I realize.
But, damn it, God, I don't have eternity.

Or do I?
    I suppose that's really what this prayer comes up to:
        Do I have eternity?
    To be convinced a little that I do,
        that you do have it with me, for me,
            would be miracle enough, I do believe,
        for then I would likely be a more patient man,
            and that, says Paul, is the first degree of love,
                and the world and I both
                      could use a great many more degrees of that.

So, God, this is what I ask,
    that you would pull off in me
        this one miracle quick enough
            to finish in my short remaining years.
Perhaps you've begun, I hope,
    by giving me pause to rest in this prayer,
        which is to rest in you.
            Thank you. Amen.

I Have Only So Much Time

I Pray To Be Steeped in Silence

Eternal God,
   since silence seems
      to be the voice of holiness,
         the only language
            you speak directly,
     then I pray
        to be steeped in it
until I fear it less
   and welcome it
      as an usher to grace,
         a narrator of sacred mysteries;
until silence cease the fretful conversations
   of my mind with too little else than itself;
until silence calm my heart to an ease,
   convene my senses to an anchored focus,
      hush my tongue to a chastened hold;
until I discern in the silence
   an answer to that necessary question
      which, for the very life of me,
         it has not yet occurred to me to ask;
until I am stretched alive
   and deep to its dimensions,
      and catch, at last and ready,
         your assuring wink at me.
            Amen.

Tutor Me Yet Again

O God of prodigious hospitality,
    the banquet of this autumn day
        is spread out in pinging crystal light,
    spans of dewy, spidery, silvery lace stretched here and there
        amongst ruby, orange, lemon, white regalia
cast about with seeming giddily generous abandon
        everywhere I look under this canopy of a cinnamony blue sky,
the air perfumed with chrysanthemum, last roses, purple grape,
        accompanied by a soft chorus of morning doves,
a ballet of prancing squirrels and butterflies in arabesques,
        a four-year-old in butt-patched denims laughing after,
tugging on his grandmother's hand like a host welcoming her
        to this drop-alive gorgeous place and time and feast.
I cannot breathe quite deeply enough to take it all in,
        though I am half-tipsy delirious in the delight of it.

But, Lord, I swear to you, and ask you why so quickly
    a shadow of familiar guilt slithers into my head,
        a voice from some past accusing place or time,
insistent as a parental storm, a child's drench in shame,
        a rasping, whispered, frightened, frightening warning
against so much enjoyment, such exuberant gladness;
        and mixed with the guilt, a sigh of aching sadness,
akin to that which often creeps in after making love,
        a puckered reminder of our fading flower mortality
as if joy, gladness, pleasure are transgressions, subtle sins,
        symptoms of self-indulgence, a blighted benevolence,
and laughter, even in delight, occasion for a later grief.

God, I cannot believe, do not want to,
    that the shadow is from your hand outstretched to chasten,
or the voice the rustle of your reckoning Spirit
    readying to snuff the joy your own creativity has kindled.

Yet, Lord, why this guilt, this sadness?
    O God, search and tutor me yet again,
        for I would not ignore these abetting signals
            lest I ignore delight's signals as well,
                and shrink for missing both,
        nor would I smudge one fingerprint of truth upon my soul
            or make a false god of what you have made
                only but a small token of your care.
Search and make me more aware
    of how easily the surround of beauty
        and unruly gorgeousness can distract me
            from the risky, bruising work of justice,
    the calloused disciplines of integrity and prayer,
        the long and wearying reach toward inclusiveness and peace.
Search and shock me again with the truth
    of how quickly the rapturous overwhelm of gladness
        the unearned magnificence and abundance of my estate
            can distance me from those who have so little to enjoy,
    who are beset by hunger, disease, and darkness,
        which you call us to remember and compassionately relieve.

Lord, I swear I am aware, a bit frightened, too,
    yet still quite aware of how short my earthly time is,
        how infinite your bounty of which I imbibe but a sip,
    but taste as the first toast of the kingdom's banquet,
        and I trust that this shadow of guilt, this whispered sadness
convey not a lasting judgment but a necessary reminder
    of the places rubbed thin between this world and the other,

Tutor Me Yet Again

  and that now's the time to be generous and just, as well as joyful
   in my brief life before night falls, gently I pray,
    and I return the breath and stardust you have lent to me.

So, I stitch together my dilemma with this shred of sagacity:
 The biggest bully is a killjoy,
  and my guilt and shame serve no neighbor well.
 I believe that you, too, must love rose and chrysanthemum,
  delight in butterflies, fat clowning squirrels,
   and leaves so gold and orange they must surprise even you,
  elate in lovers tickled breathless, children fresh as sass,
   spiders spinning silk, prophets who can laugh,
    elders soaked in hard scrabble time,
     wrung out in wrinkles, wit and wisdom.

And I know very well, Lord,
 I can never repay a tad of the bounty of this life you give,
  but never mind, that matters not, for your summons is
   to share it fairly with every least, last one,
 rejoicing all the while, for you have eased the burden
  of my indebtedness in this dawn of revelation
 that you rejoice, too, and take delight in all of this
  that overflows from you
   to overflow in my delight in you.

Now I do rejoice to lift, on a waft of perfumed air,
 in the pinging chalice of this crystal-lighted space,
  a glad, brash morning toast to you,
   this stumble of quiet ecstasy
    and quite unutterable gratitude
     for your quite unfathomable grace.
     Amen.

Tutor Me Yet Again

Go With Me, God

O God,
    though sometimes the flight
        is several anniversaries prolonged,
   mostly it's a too-quick, easy trip
       to where anger takes us,
where searing words spew squadrons of sparks
      to char everything in all directions,
          past and future, near and far,
where toxic, gray gloom of accusations
      blurs every eye, dulls every ear,
where both sides slip-slide off and away
      to retreats cold as never,
         sullen as mud,
            limed in oozy self-pity
               and vinegary rebuttals.

O God,
   once upon a long time ago,
      it seemed, or felt at least
         (and sometimes even now),
that anger has its own demonic source,
    a momentum all its own,
erupting in us like a volcanic flood,
    vaporizing our better angels
       in its fiery blitz,
         sweeping us along,
as if we have no power to resist
     yet perversely enjoy the thrill
        (as I admit I do, in that momentary,
           brutish adrenaline rush).

Go With Me, God

Now I know anger differently:
    It's the marrow and the urge of me,
my repeated acting out of Eden's fall,
    a persistent, long-misguided claim
        to some primal, still-wished-for control;
a childish tantrum over-reach
    toward rights and righteousness
        really not mine in the least,
just my illusions, which,
    try as I might to make them do,
        cannot cover my abounding,
            nagging mortal nakedness.

O God,
    it is cut-off lonely there,
        where anger take us, then leaves,
this land of truly wasted time, and life.
    Come, now and find me.

O God,
    I know it's a long, hard trip
        out of anger and retreat
to any repair of the breech,
    any beginning degree
        of a longed-for intimacy.

Go with me, with us,
    as you went with Adam and Eve
        and all the us's ever since,
some to healing avail.

Go With Me, God

Go with me, God,
   through honest self-knowledge
      to a proportioned humility,
   from fevered accusation
      to accurate apology,
   from delicious aggrievement
      to a shared cup of forgiveness,
   from stunting addiction to my biases
      to crediting the other's side,
         a glimpsing of the larger, inclusive view
            seen by four eyes or more, instead of two.

Go with me, God,
   on this long trip
      of listening and letting go,
   all the winding ways
      toward seeing myself truly,
         seeing where I am
            and who, and how I got here,
      seeing all my misbegotten pride,
         all my blighting misperception
            of others, and mostly of you.

Go with me, God,
   on this walk on the narrow ridge,
      enabling me to stand my ground
         without betraying it in passivity
            or disguising it in manipulating,
               or in false modesty,
                   an hypocrisy worse than blind pride;
      to stand my ground humbly
         so as not to deny others theirs,
            or invading theirs with ridicule.

Go With Me, God

Grant me courage to say what I mean
    and honestly mean what I say,
        without judging what others say or mean,
    and so making myself trustworthy,
        transforming anger into the energy
            to make new things possible.

O God,
    it is not just a way back that I'm praying for,
        but a way to a different place
            than habit has worn out,
                a home I never had before.
    I sense it takes a trip of many turns, returns,
        and many years to make, remake,
            and make again.

Go with me,
    to keep me from getting lost,
        or being too reluctantly ashamed
    to take the first demanding steps
        that will be the beginning now
            of that lifetime journey
                to the self I so passionately long to be,
                    to those I love and lost awhile,
                and so to those in the shimmering web
                    of this human family I'm in for good,
                and so to you,
                    who, I am praying,
                        waits close to welcome
                            and go limping home with me.
                        Amen.

Go With Me, God

Let Me Make Something of This Loss

God . . . damn this pain,
    this shroud of darkness,
        this gaping emptiness,
    damn this sneering ache inside,
        this death of one I love,
            cry for, whisper after,
                can no longer engage . . .
    save in the wandering graze
        of my too-mortal memory,
            and so miss as if life itself
                has withered pale away.

God . . . damn this dog-breathed death
    that snatched away this precious one,
        and left its cruel claw marks
            on near everything.
    How dare the sky stretch its jay-blue wings another day!
        How dare the sun not shut its saucer eye,
            and beguiling stars not pull down their shades!
    Trees should droop now on,
        lovers stand cold apart,
            all music become a requiem,
                all laughter turn to a lament,
                      all talk stutter to a sheepish halt,
                          and squealing children shush to baffled silence!

God, does no one, does nothing, know what I know now?
    Or does everyone, everything know what I do not?
        Is this some minor loss, one note missed in a symphony?
            No! Surely it's the end of song itself!

Let Me Make Something of This Loss

>That's what I know. That's my truth, the throb of what I feel.
>>That's the stagger of it, the cramp, the whole of what is real.
>God, save me from glib comforters who have no sense of that.
>>What I want is to know they have some glimmer of my grief.
>>>I want to see it in their eyes, the tremble of their chin,
>>>>no smooth words, no easy reassurances, false promises,
>>>>>just eyes, and a hand to hold.

God, there is no one
>to occupy this emptiness.
>>No one. Not even you. Not yet.
>>>For this grief is mine . . .
>>>>that's half the snarl of it.
>In the pain is something
>>as troubling as the loss itself:
>>>It is the *mine*-ness of it.
>I am left to bear the grief, know the loss, and yet
>>you know the strange twists of this human heart . . .
>>>I feel something somehow noble
>>>>in the bearing, in the knowing,
>>>>>in the half-proud mine-ness of it,
>>>>>>the center I've made myself of things.

Still . . . God could you be precisely in the bearing, in the knowing?
>Are these the traces of grace to deepen my grief
>>past a wallow in self-pity, deeper than a flirt with guilt,
>>>down to a truly staunch compassion,
>>>>a kind of joining of the muddling human family,
>>>>>and a keener awareness of the lengths to which you go
>>>>>>to save us from ourselves—
>>>>>>>with our necessary assist?

Let Me Make Something of This Loss

I confess it. I am not the one who died.
   Had the choice been mine as to which of us would,
      perhaps I would have offered to die instead,
         for I love as fully as I can,
            and yet . . . perhaps I would not have chosen so.
      Something deep in me is glad to be alive.

So, Lord, save me as well from pretentious grieving,
   from the affectation and self-importance lurking in loss
     that, with the accompaniment of attention and admiration,
        foolishly tries to gild the emptiness without touching it
          or transforming it—for any of us.
  If gladness to be alive
     is no more than a way to deaden my fear of death,
       then that's the real emptiness, isn't it?
         God, you know . . .
            you know . . .
               Comfort comes closer
                  with my knowing that you know.

God, gather my tears, my fears, my lashing out and in,
  and translate them into the prayers I mean.
     What I mean, what I ask, what I need,
       what I scream, cry, beg, even demand,
         is that you move into my emptiness
           with mercy, with healing, with hope,
              with something stronger than my fear,
                with your presence.
                  Please!

Let Me Make Something of This Loss

Lord, stay with me, for only you can fill this emptiness.
   Bit by bit, moment by moment, for as long as it takes,
      as long as I have, as deep as my need, as high as my hope,
         fill this emptiness with your presence.
            I ask for no more.
   Save that you take to heart
      this one I've loved long since and lost awhile.
         Grant her peace, and joy,
            a corner in your kingdom,
               a worthy challenge, an endless growing.

Strength, Lord, I ask this smidgen more;
   strength to live with these answerless questions
      and hope to move with less fear into the uncertain future.
   Let me never again leave
      so much of my truth unspoken,
         so much of my love unlived,
            so much of my dream for the "us" of life undared,
   let so many possibilities for joy shrivel from inattention,
      so much of faith curdle into timidity,
         so much of beauty be aborted by indifference,
            so much of hope fade for want of courage.
   God, bless me into forgiving this one I love and see no more.
      Bless me into seeing her real and thanking and forgiving her,
         lest I lose her in idealizing or self-pitying complaining.

I swear I will wrestle with you
   until you so bless me, and forgive me.
      Comfort rises warm in the cold of me
         because I can so wrestle
            and you promise to so bless and forgive.
               So we go on . . . limping on . . . hoping on . . .
                  every step, at last, a testament of gratitude.

Let Me Make Something of This Loss

God, please, help me!
   Please, let me make something of this loss,
      something strong and right and brave,
         something faithful, something full of laughter again,
           of blue skies, of songs and winking stars,
              and trustworthy friendships,
                 of my being a trustworthy friend
                    of others,
                      of you.

Help me on this long, bumpy, pockmarked road to glory.
   I passionately hope my loved one watches for me there.
      My hope is rooted in your promise.
         Let it carry me with you
            through the long days
               and nights ahead.

And now, Mother and Father of us all,
   grace to help me fold my frantic, weary wings
      beneath your enfolding, eternal ones,
         and rest there in peace this night,
            as my loved one rests eternally in you.
               Amen.

Let Me Make Something of This Loss

Teach Me How to Die

O my Lord,
    in the soft twilight the crickets are singing
        toward the coming night and summer's end.
    It's a curiously comforting song,
        yet melancholy as well,
            a soul-tugging reminder
                of another coming night,
                      quite another season's end.
O God,
    Giver of both beginnings and endings, life and death.
        this cricket-stirred prayer
            lifts from my deepest secret heart,
                where fear stalks in the long shadows,
                    shivering my courage, chilling my dreams,
                        dousing any embers of certainty.

Teach me, please, how to die!
    Not that I want to any time soon,
        or exactly need to know before doing it,
            or that I won't learn on my very human own,
                but that is why I pray, plead, now:
                    Please, teach me how to die!
    On my human own is an eternity
        from learning rightly how.

Teach me to trust, at least a little more,
    that your grace and providence
        extends even to your gift of death,
            so I will become a little less afraid,

though I confess I still wish a gentle passing,
    a brief contraction or two,
        if it's at all like birth,
    and the assurance that someone
        will be there to receive me
            on my trembling arrival.

Teach me the ways of courage past bravado,
    that whether death come gently or harshly,
        be brief in coming, or lingering,
    I will be able to face it
        without flinching or complaining—
            except perhaps an excusable little.

Teach me to be graceful in this present
    as even now my horizons shrink
        and my dreams fade like a favorite shirt,
            so others will grieve but once,
                only for my exit, not the way of it.

Teach me gratitude, as I reflect in the mirror of this gathering dusk,
    for all I have received, if never receiving a dram more:
        the caress of all the years of life,
            of all the precious lives and loves,
                beauty and blessedness,
                      memories of their joys flitting like butterflies
                          through these days, keepsakes of resurrections.

Teach me, in this season of my life,
    more of the faithful lesson of the crickets,
        and of Christ, if that's not too great a stretch,
    that as death buzzes like a fly around and in my head,
        detonates an awful pain within my heart,
            turns breathing into a slow gasp,

Teach Me How to Die

I'll find strength enough at least
    to hum a few notes of a hymn,
        whisper a bit of some psalm, a snatch of prayer,
    wisdom enough to smile,
        presence enough to speak my love for those
            who have borne and enriched me;
    find gratitude enough to forgive and ask to be forgiven
        for the smudges and the wounds
            left by my legacy;
    yet grace enough to celebrate in my soul
        at that last moment
            the good-glad inheritance left to them
                whom I see, even now, in the faces,
                    the lives, loves, and gifts
                        I'm blooded and bonded to.

Teach me, Lord, more of love, the secret of the crickets' song,
    that amidst any sadness or regret at endings,
        I may sing now, and then, if not forevermore,
            that song of comfort to myself,
                and more, to those I'll love long,
                      long past the beating of my heart
                          where they reside, as they reside with you
    to whom I commit them now, and then, and always,
        as I do myself, seizing for them and myself
            the hope set before us in Jesus,
                and knowing the song
                    I am learning to sing is yours,
                        O God of grace and of all creatures
                          great and small.
                            Amen.

Teach Me How to Die

I Watch, Wondering, For You

God . . . it's morning again.
   The tide of light rises,
      slides down the walls,
         across the ceiling, into my eyes,
            purging the darkness,
               probing relentlessly into resistant corners,
                  slowly smoothing the crinkles of sleep.
   I watch, wondering if a single breaker of light
      will curl into my heart this time,
         chasing away the shadows left over
            from so many splotch-strewn yesterdays,
               the stalking nightmares of so many midnights . . .

I watch, wondering, for you.
   I wait still for one word from you,
      one clear, no-mistaking word
         addressed to me alone,
compelling beyond any compromise,
   certain beyond any doubting,
      assuring beyond any confusion.

You know there are many who are so sure.
   You know, as well, I am not one of them.
      I anguish over why, and you know that, too.
   I am blest, yes, beyond all telling of it,
      and all thanking, all deserving,
         but not sure beyond all puzzling
            about who's the one who blesses,
      and the why of that as well. Why me?

I Watch, Wondering, For You

So I watch and wait, and weary of you . . .
    Sometimes . . . often . . . of you, yes
        but mostly of myself,
            this heady, self-absorbed questioning.

Now another day knocks,
    eager-knuckled, shiny-faced, insistent.
Yet, wisps of yesterday still clutter my thoughts,
    debris as after a parade,
        to promote my self-importance, my apparent virtue,
            my being there for whoever asks,
                mouthing more wisdom than is in my heart,
                    more encouragement than I feel,
                        more answers than honest truth allows.
Assuming I need more than you,
    I am too ambitious, too quietly demanding
        that my love be reimbursed in multiples,
            my goodness be recognized and lauded.
    No wonder my mouth is sour now,
        my body stiff, my spirit weary of its duplicities,
            yet, grateful for its somewhat authenticity.
For I am here yet, still here, longingly here, laughingly here.

And you? You are still here, too, surely.
    You must be for I still address you, the haunt of my life.
    Evidently you are able still
        to turn the little loaves and fish I am
            into food for some others,
        and that would be the wonder as well.
For that, too, happened yesterday in the light
    that broke and climbed in the eyes of those
        who looked unflinchingly back into mine.

I Watch, Wondering, For You

I forget so easily but remember now,
     the kingdom is in our midst . . .
          Where else?

Now, God, having niggled you
     with my carping wish
          for one word from you,
               one clear, no-mistaking word
                    addressed to me alone,
I am left to trust that what is clear
     is that you have no word for me *alone*,
          probably for no one alone,
               creating us as you have
                    for each other.
No word except this usual, inarguable one:
     "Get up and go. Begin again.
          The next one you meet,
               and honestly engage,
                    will bear to you
                         my presence."
                         All right! I hear. I go.
A particle of light
     has pierced my heart . . . again.
          'Tis enough!
               I am yours as long
                    as there is light . . .
                         any . . . at all.
                              Amen.

I Watch, Wondering, For You

THE REV. DR. THEODORE W. LODER has been the Senior Minister of one of Philadelphia's most unusual churches, the First United Methodist Church of Germantown (known locally as FUMCOG), for almost thirty-eight years. This thriving, ethnically-mixed metropolitan congregation of over one thousand members has affectionately been labeled "The Oddball Church" by *Philadelphia Inquirer Magazine*. With imagination and intensity, Loder has led FUMCOG to the forefront of artistic endeavors, political activism, and social justice. His congregation has been a Public Sanctuary Church, a founding church of the Covenant Against Apartheid in South Africa, a Reconciling Congregation that advocates for the rights of homosexual persons, and the founder of a major medical mission in a depressed area of Philadelphia. In addition, the church has a mission project in Fondwa, Haiti, and supports "For the Love of Children" (FLOC) Pre-School Program in Johannesburg, South Africa.

Loder's own social action grows out of a long history of involvement in social causes, including marching with Dr. Martin Luther King, Jr., in the sixties. Loder is co-founder of Metropolitan Career Center (a job-training program for high school drop-outs); co-founder of Plowshares (a non-profit housing renovation corporation); and co-founder of Urban Resource Development Corporation (an ecumenical effort to rehabilitate abandoned houses). He has also served on the Philadelphia Mayor's Advisory Commission for Children and Families.

For many people who have "given up" on the church, Loder brings a breath of fresh air. His blend of scholarship (cum laude degree from Yale Divinity School, a university fellow of the Yale Graduate School, and two honorary doctorates) and creativity (named by the *National Observer* as "One of America's Outstanding Creative Preachers") stimulate his refreshing openness to hard questions, to change, to relevance, to justice, and to joy.

Made in the USA
Monee, IL
08 April 2020